MRAC

W9-AOL-060

THE BREAKS

THE BREAKS

Julietta Singh

COFFEE HOUSE PRESS
Minneapolis
2021

Copyright © 2021 by Julietta Singh
Cover design by June Park
Book design by Rachel Holscher
Author photograph © Chase Joynt

"What People Do" is from *Words Under the Words: Selected Poems* by
Naomi Shihab Nye, copyright © 1995. Reprinted with permission of
Far Corner Books.

Coffee House Press books are available to the trade through our pri-
mary distributor, Consortium Book Sales & Distribution, cbsd.com
or (800) 283-3572. For personal orders, catalogs, or other information,
write to info@coffeehousepress.org.

Coffee House Press is a nonprofit literary publishing house. Support
from private foundations, corporate giving programs, government
programs, and generous individuals helps make the publication of our
books possible. We gratefully acknowledge their support in detail in
the back of this book.

LIBRARY OF CONGRESS CATALOGING-IN-PUBLICATION DATA

Names: Singh, Julietta, 1976– author.
Title: The breaks / Julietta Singh.
Description: Minneapolis : Coffee House Press, 2021. | Summary:
    "An epistolary essay about race, inheritance, and mothering at
    the end of the world"— Provided by publisher.
Identifiers: LCCN 2021007841 | ISBN 9781566896160 (trade
    paperback) | ISBN 9781566896252 (ebook)
Subjects: LCSH: Singh, Julietta, 1976– | East Indians—United
    States—Biography. | Mother and child—United States. |
    Racism—United States. | Queer theory—United States.
Classification: LCC E184.E2 b .S56 2021 | DDC 305.800973—dc23
LC record available at https://lccn.loc.gov/2021007841

PRINTED IN THE UNITED STATES OF AMERICA

28 27 26 25 24 23 22 21   1 2 3 4 5 6 7 8

THE BREAKS

In the run-up to Thanksgiving last year, you learned a whitewashed story at school about how the first peoples of this land were happy to give their sacred spaces to the consumptive force of European men in the name of civilization and progress. You came home from school and unzipped your backpack, revealing with artistic pride a picture book you had colored and stapled yourself. Your kindergarten teacher had asked you to color in a little Native American girl, then a Native American boy, followed by a pilgrim girl and boy, each one garbed in their traditional attire. I admired the craft of your book, a swell of parental pride coursing through me as I witnessed the evidence of my progeny doing and making things in the world beyond me. And I relished that you had colored all four children Brown like you.

As you flipped through the pages of your book, you narrated a sad story about how much the pilgrims had suffered when they arrived on this land. I felt a surge in my body, an immediate, unstoppable need to explain the other forms of suffering elided by this disturbingly singular narrative. I described some of the impacts of this arrival on Indigenous peoples—the European theft of their autonomies, cultures, languages, and lands. I explained that colonial practices dramatically changed how humans live in relation to this land. And I told you that this historical moment of colonial contact was crucial to understanding how we arrived at the global ecological crisis we face today.

I will never forget the way you looked at me then, your head slightly tilted to one side, your eyes wide in bewilderment. We were sitting on the landing at the top of the apartment stairs, the contents of your backpack scattered around us. *This is* not *what my teacher told us,* you said with unmistakable agitation. I knew that for the first time you were confronting the existence of conflicting worldviews, a vital gulf between your formal education and your maternal one. *That's okay,* I said. *My job as your mother is to tell you these stories differently, and to tell you other stories that don't get told at school.* I pressed on to explain that history is a story based on a version of the past. *Can you hear the word* story *in* history, I asked? You nodded slowly, a little body in deep rumination. *These stories need to be told from the perspectives of those who have been most damaged by history. These other stories,* I said, *can teach us how to keep living.*

From the onset of your public education, you have been learning what it means to be American through a manicured version of history that keeps European whiteness at its center. This form of education willfully forgets the lives that were destroyed, the bodies that were brutalized, and the cultures and traditions that were abolished or displaced to establish that center space. It tells you a singular and continuous narrative of Western capitalist expansion, obscuring the bleak fact that much of what we call "progress" has been a direct and unrelenting line to the wholesale destruction of the earth. Against this obliterating narrative, I glean from the fragments in an attempt to teach us otherwise. I scramble to harvest alternative histories omitted by the textbooks, the histories of those who have faced annihilation and lived toward survival.

Learning to mother at the end of the world is an infinite toggle between wanting to make you feel safe and needing you to know that the earth and its inhabitants are facing a catastrophic crisis. This morning, you went off to school to learn discipline, to hone your reading and writing skills, to study official state history. I am at my desk sipping tea, turning over words. The birds are chirping outside my window. You, me, the birds. We are all creatures living as though we have a future, as though tomorrow will continue to resemble today. Meanwhile, plans are being devised to drive the marketplace forward when the earth's nonrenewable resources are exhausted. Scientists and businessmen are plotting to colonize the moon in a relentless drive to create an alternative human habitat when this one can no longer foster us. There is no consideration of ceasing extraction, only a maniacal mission to discover other worlds to plunder.

When the earth is rendered uninhabitable, when extractive capitalism leads to wholesale ecological collapse, we will not be chosen for this new other-planetary world. We, along with nearly everyone else, will be left in ecological destruction to scavenge what we can from the wreckage, or to perish. The truth is I am glad not to be among the chosen ones. I know in my body the cost of "discovering new worlds," the brutal violence that accompanies the colonial mission. No, I do not want to leave this planet. What I want is another world. And when I say *another world*, I mean this one, toppled and reborn.

Another Thanksgiving is upon us, and this year you inform me that your first-grade class will soon be studying Pocahontas. You ask me earnestly whether we might watch the Disney movie together. Intuiting my hesitation, you add that Pocahontas comes from the land near where we now live, and that she is a *superimportant person*. I concede to your request, knowing you will see this film sooner or later, and finding myself oddly curious about how Disney has rendered this history.

In preparation for our date, we slice apples, pour chamomile tea, and fill bowls with popcorn before climbing into my bed to watch under the covers. Early in the film, you declare that Pocahontas reminds you of yourself, and I ask you how you see a resemblance. Eager to keep your attention on the movie, you briefly list her kindness and her connection with nature. Then, in a fabulous offhanded gesture that makes me laugh, you add that Pocahontas's hair, which is long, immaculate, and shining black, is quite similar to your own short, ever-disheveled, and unmistakably brown hair.

Moments later—on the heels of your declarative affiliation with Pocahontas—you say, for the first time in your life, *I wish I was white.* I hit the space bar on the laptop to pause the film. I feel like I'm sliding through time, careening into transmutation. Thirty-five years ago, I too was a little girl wishing for whiteness. I am astonished by the twinning, even though I know intellectually that a childhood wish for whiteness is as mundane as it is predictable. Still, in that split second I want to look into your eyes, our eyes, and say, *I have always loved you, little misfit.*

Instead, I ask an inane question: *Why do you feel this way?* You respond without hesitation, bluntly, *Because I want to be one of the good guys.* I remind you that the only expressly "bad guy" we've seen so far in the film is the white Ratcliffe. But I know you are intuiting and absorbing the representation of the "savage" that the film propagates, and so while there is one "bad" white man in this narrative, the "uncivilized" ways of the Indigenous peoples of this film are presented as the real problem. In other words, you are reading the film through its own disturbing lens: the white man is fundamentally good if we can just beat off the one bad seed, and the Indigenous peoples are inherently misguided and belligerent, even while we are given permission to love the girl who dared to love a white man.

How to explain all this to you? How to say in simple terms that we are steeped in layers of ideology that make up a collective sense of goodness, beauty, and civility? To explain that these dominant narratives come to inform, if not dictate, what we desire and how we live our most intimate lives. I cannot shield you from these structures of belief or their profound and abiding effects on you. But I can complicate and unearth them with you. Indeed, my role as your mother may be nothing more than an endless task of reading narratives against the grain, of resisting the mainstream's consumptive ease.

When the film is done, we turn out the lights to fall asleep together and our ritual unfolds. I whisper, *I love you for always. You're my favorite thing.* You respond, *Tell me a story, Amma.* Then, often together, we say, *Once upon a time, a long, long time ago* . . . before I break into a fantastical story that you expect me, night after night, to invent for you on the spot.

Once upon a time, a long, long time ago, there was a magical little girl—
You interrupt me promptly and insist, *No! Not magical, Amma!*
So, I begin again . . . *There was an* ordinary *little girl* . . .
And then, frustrated with my easy adjectival foreclosures, you interrupt to assert that I should not *make the story so obvious* . . .

Who is the teacher and who is the student in this elementary pedagogy? In the end, it is you who schools me—to always complicate the story, to never prescribe, never reduce. There is infinite promise in this teaching. I hold the lesson in my body.

On the sixth day of a nine-day work trip—the longest period I have been away from you—I FaceTime home and find you deeply engaged in an act of fruit sculpting. You tell me you are making a Powhatan village. The Powhatan people are represented by banana slices, and apple skins make up their shelters. Off to the side of the village, you have crafted colonial ships by slicing kiwis in half, gutting their insides, and attaching the skins to the little fruit boats to serve as sails. You have created rough waters out of banana peels, and a wall of carved-apple manatees that surrounds the kiwi ships on three sides.

What's happening in this scene? I ask.
The rough waters and manatees are pushing the Europeans back home, you reply earnestly.

I am blown away to witness this art-making against the state, this anticolonial fruit installation that is also a fantasy of organically reversing history. What I love most is that in your historical revisioning, you move us beyond the subjugated histories of Indigenous resistance to colonial force. Instead, you turn your attention to the sea, letting it emerge as an actor in the opposition to the colonial mission. Your artwork veers me away from the anthropocentric position, carefully and imaginatively invoking what the earth itself might desire.

Last year, as we walked to school hand in hand through the lush green streets of Richmond, Virginia, you asked me with stark curiosity whether you would have been a slave had you lived here in another time. The question did not come as an absolute surprise, because I knew you had been studying Abraham Lincoln and Thomas Jefferson in kindergarten. Only months into your formal education, and you were already immersed in a top-down history that tells you Black folks became free through the noble gestures of white presidential slave owners. This history slyly refuses to include the resistance from below that has always made freedom possible. It is a history that will not tell you how hard and through what means Black and Brown people have fought to be free, how crushing the blows of European "progress" have been to those subjected to its force.

Your question was hard for me to answer because its limbs extended in so many directions, because it required not a single answer, not a reductive *no* or *yes,* but a careful inventory of moving bodies. Some of those bodies came with colonial minds, some were "discovered" here and brutally eradicated or displaced, some were captured from elsewhere and forced across the ocean, and others came from distant lands to save or improve their lives. At its root, your question was a way of asking where your body fits into the racial economy of this nation. And the answer to that question must necessarily be a dynamic one.

I tightened my grip on your hand, slowed our pace, and drew you close. I told you that people like us did not live here during the time of slavery. But already I was wondering about the words I used—*people like us.* Who was this *us* I had summoned to make sense of things for you? At the time, I had undoubtedly meant those critically impacted by the force and manipulation of British colonialism in India. But my utterance also implicated the Jews who were exterminated and those who narrowly escaped the Nazi camps. Our blood is laced with modern histories of unbelievable violence. It is a strange and hybrid brew that you will feel in your body across your life, as I have always felt it in mine.

Our particular histories are those of imperial conquest, mass extermination, and nearly unimaginable forms of racial and religious violence. But here in America, it is toward the local histories of genocide, slavery, forced religious and cultural conversion, and internment that we must reach in solidary. Each of us who emerges from the subjugated ends of history, who stands outside whiteness but is also saturated by its power, shares something not only at the surface of our bodies but also deep within them.

I am writing to you, and to future you. I am writing to the six-year-old girl you are now, the one who both insists on her unequivocal need for my body and loves to perform her independence from me.

You slide your hands along my skin, expressing your endless love for my body as you lock your arms around my waist. I am busy with some task—an email, the groceries, a lecture that needs to be written—and when I try to unlatch, you strike a dramatic tone and declare, *But I need your body to live!* We both laugh, understanding that in this fantasy you are a helpless infant and I a gigantic breast, the wellspring of your survival. You have outgrown my womb and my milk, but my body remains your target. A deeply desired dwelling place, a fantasy of origin and endless return.

Yet in the social world, you are all independence and moxie, a creature that appears to have sprung autonomously, fully formed. You toddled, then dashed, now saunter into social spaces and make your presence known. At the farmers market, you help the farmers organize and sell their produce. At the grocery, you join your "coworkers," chatting with the employees as you help bag groceries or work the customer service desk. You don't always mind your parents nearby but make clear your strong preference that we kick back at a distance, let you navigate your own social relations. You both need me to live and love to not need me at all.

I am writing also to the becoming-being that you are, the one who will face a world in ruin and undoubtedly wonder over my place in all this destruction.

Over half a century ago, James Baldwin repeatedly wrote and tore up drafts of a letter penned to his nephew and namesake until he was able to articulate the plain, pitiless fact that the younger James would face profound struggle *for no other reason* but the fact of his Blackness. More recently, Ta-Nehisi Coates followed Baldwin to elucidate for his son the brutal truth of state violence inflicted against Black bodies. It is no coincidence that both Baldwin and Coates have felt an urgency to write to fifteen-year-old boys tipping into manhood, their Black paternal mouths spilling with revolutionary promise as they equip their boys to face a criminal justice system designed to exploit and devour them.

I write to you with a different urgency. I write not with the immediate fear that you will be gunned down by police in the streets, or that you will be metabolized by the prison industrial complex, but with an adjacent set of fears about being a Brown girl in a country that thinks and feels race through a sharp binary. I write with an impossible desire to prepare you for political and ecological catastrophe. I write because the burden of history—the indispensable need to keep us all from coming apart—keeps falling on the shoulders of girls and women of color. I write because, as mother and daughter, we are unmistakably entwined, and because I know—which is to say I feel in the most microbial registers of my body—that the shape of our entwinement will need to be radically reformed as we fight global patriarchy, extractive capitalism, and indiscriminate planetary destruction.

I recently stumbled on a documentary called *Warrior Women* that centers on Madonna Thunder Hawk, an Indigenous leader, mother, and member of the American Indian Movement (AIM). In the 1970s, Thunder Hawk established a grassroots school devised to educate the children of AIM, calling it the We Will Remember Survival School. Generations of Indigenous children had been forcibly subjected to Indigenous boarding schools, an assimilationist education that removed children from their families, cultures, and languages, brutally punishing them for "transgressing" into their Native ways. Against an educational system that sought to eradicate indigeneity from the "New World," Thunder Hawk offered a decolonial education that returned children to their Indigenous worldviews. Emphasizing the subjects of land, law, and spirituality, the school not only taught what had been stripped from the children through colonial indoctrination but cultivated in them the tools they would need to fight the state for their rights and freedoms. How to care for and be cared for by the land. How to understand and navigate a legal system bent on manipulating and destroying their communities. How to commune with their ancestors, to walk a spiritual path that enabled children to remember what was already within and around them. By outright refusing state-sanctioned knowledge, Thunder Hawk's Survival School made Indigenous education an act of revolutionary survival.

The documentary found me one morning while I was writing about race, motherhood, and extinction. It came to me by way of my inbox, a promotional announcement that sprang up on my screen. Resonant as it was with my morning musings, I responded immediately to the email with a request to view the film, and promised the distributor I would promptly ask my university library to purchase it for their video collection. I watched the documentary with a thirst, a relish. It articulated through the history of Indigenous struggle what I desired for us now on a global scale: a form of education that would return us to something that was being stripped away; a survival school that would teach us all how to live amidst and against the belligerent exploitation of the earth.

Being as diasporic as we are, I find I have no traditional knowledge to bestow upon you, no single spiritual or cultural heritage that will reach back to precolonial ways of being and knowing. Lacking these forms of heritage, I turn intuitively to language and theory. I teach you by attending to what is effaced by the language we speak, what is rendered lifeless in this linguistic worldview, and what is made to sound supreme. I draw from thinkers like Mel Y. Chen, who illuminates how what is bestowed with life and lifelessness on a scale of animacy has everything to do with racial hierarchies and systemic oppressions. Chen asks us to think about who counts as human, which humans are less worthy than others, what is perceived as vital and what is not imbued with life at all. I let theory guide us to make sense of this world, to imagine and articulate another one in which we are no longer made to live in isolation from the world that has always created and sustained us.

In *Braiding Sweetgrass,* Robin Wall Kimmerer dwells on her ancestral language, Potawatomi, which articulates everything as alive and does not divide the world into binaries such as male and female. It is a language of interconnection, one that does not conceive the world in terms of separation and hierarchy. She writes: *The animacy of the world is something we already know, but the language of animacy teeters on extinction—not just for Native peoples, but for everyone.* Kimmerer reminds us of the power of language to shape how we understand the world, and the loss of interconnectedness that accompanies learning to speak a language like English. Our interconnectedness quickly disappears when we are steeped in a linguistic frame where the human reigns supreme. This language we have inherited has tried hard to divide the world into living and nonliving things, into a scale of hierarchized animate life on the one hand, and a so-called inanimate world ripe for exploitation and extraction on the other.

As children, Kimmerer reminds us, we are born knowing the world is infinitely alive and lively. We are all trained over time to make the cut, to sever the world into animate and inanimate life. We become educated—"civilized"— through a process that increasingly refuses life to other living entities. Kimmerer asks us to enliven and be enlivened by the languages we have and the languages we seek to learn. I am watching you begin to lose this sense of the world, become immersed in the imperial way of knowing. While I may not have an ancestral language to come home to or to teach you, I love to play with the one we share. To unmake and remake this language, to loosen its strangleholds while collaborating with it in the hopes of making us all more free. I try to teach you against my own teaching, to reanimate a world of flourishing animacies I have almost lost.

Kimmerer, once more: *To become native to this place, if we are to survive here, and our neighbors too, our work is to learn to speak the grammar of animacy, so that we might truly be at home.* I can't help but linger on this notion of being truly at home, because while I understand it conceptually, I have never fully felt it. Not on the stolen lands upon which I was born. Not in the imposing beige brick home where I was raised on the banks of the Assiniboine River. Not on the soil of India, where my father was born, nor in my mother's Europe. Not here in the United States, where I stumbled away from Canada one day and somehow never returned. I have only just begun to feel this home-feeling with you, with your father, in our everyday acts of collective world-making. For the first time, I wonder whether I need to stop drifting, not so much in body as in spirit, to let myself *become native to this place.* To *live* here, right where we are, and to articulate that living by learning who and how and when and why we have all come to live here, to belong here. To witness everything around us as alive, and to become part of that liveliness.

In *Warrior Women*, we learn that Thunder Hawk was not the easiest mother, not *maternal* in any conventional sense, busy keeping her people alive and ensuring the younger ones would know how to fight and persist. This is an enduring maternity—the mother who gives over new life, then keeps laboring for the survival of those abused and discarded by the state. There is a clear sense of pain in the interview with Thunder Hawk's daughter, Marcy Gilbert, who understands the urgency of her mother's work but can't help but long for another kind of maternal nurturing. I understand Marcy's longing, having myself been mothered by an unrelenting activist for whom the preservation of urban forests and the dismantling of factory farms were as vital to her as her children. You can't fault that dedication, because as a daughter you know your mother's renegade action is in service of life itself. But it doesn't stop the longing, the thick feeling inside you that wants to take another shape but can't find the proper form. By the end of the documentary, Marcy has emerged as an Indigenous leader in her own right, a food activist who understands nourishment and sustenance as core to Indigenous resistance and survival. We are each our mother's daughters, let loose in the world to heal and to offer healing, to build from the weight and wonder of the women who made us and who let us go.

However we approach it—through scientific evidence, observation, or instinct—there is no doubt left that your lifetime will be characterized by the urgent pursuit of human survival, the absolute need to overthrow our current forms of living. What we face is not a looming ethical question about how the global climate crisis will affect future generations. It is a crisis of the here and now. If we hope to survive not only as subjugated communities but as a life-form among other life-forms, this survival requires an unequivocal turn toward unacknowledged, discarded, and subaltern histories of collective resistance. Through the embrace of revolutionary women, we can remember how to live, breathe, and battle systems driven by endless subjugation, consumption, and resource extraction at the expense of life itself. Against our colonial educations, we can begin to feel toward a collective survival school set against a system destroying our chances at human life on earth. We need to study and absorb other ways of life and living, learning from those who have come before us. Rather than submit to a fantasy of simple return, we might use this learned knowledge to create imaginative political space for other ways of life that have not yet been lived. Whatever paths we take need to lead toward meeting this devastation head-on, hurling our bodies against the destroying forces in service of all life, and offering ourselves back to this beautiful, ravaged earth.

I admit that at a conceptual level there is a crucial part of me that wants to throw in the towel on human life. To say, once and for all, *Yes, let us humans all become extinct, and let the world live on without us.* Yet motherhood complicates this conceptual willingness. Because there is a body—your body—that I cannot bear to lose. A body I refuse to surrender to capitalist ruin.

In your infancy, I once staged a pitiful story-time walkout at the local public library when the librarian read a Thanksgiving story to the children that represented the national holiday as a tribute to the *collaboration* between Indigenous peoples and European colonizers. My walkout was, of course, ridiculous. I threw up my arms, grabbed your tiny body, and left the library in a huff. But this did nothing by way of explaining to the librarian, or the roomful of white American mothers, why I found the story so misleading. Or why this kind of historical rendering might actually be causing us *all* profound harm.

The college campus where I work was recently plastered with Patriot Front stickers that read *America: Conquered Not Stolen*. Confronted by the stickers as I walked to class, I found myself wondering over the difference the white supremacists desired to make between *conquest* and *theft*. Both seemed to be acts of taking what does not belong to you and making it yours. When I arrived in class, I posed the question to my students, asking whether they could parse the difference. Weighing the conqueror against the thief, we surmised that from the logic of the stickers, *conquest* was seen as noble, while *theft* an act of cowardice. *Conquest* implies military force, and with it a righteousness in the taking; it is the act of proving yourself capable of breaking another body (or people, or region, or nation), and of executing enduring control.

Thieving, I thought, seemed like the more nuanced and dynamic act, an act that might be engaged in simply to sustain oneself or one's people. I couldn't help but feel there was so much more potential in the figure of the thief, so much more capacity for an ethical life. *If I had to choose*, I told my students, *I choose the thief.*

After school, my eyes are fixed on your endlessly moving body, running, sliding, kicking, dangling in a vast architectural web that has been newly installed on the playground. Almost always, you are in a sea of boys, not only holding your own but inventing the playful scene. You concoct the game spontaneously, then summon a motley crew of others to join. As I watch you, I overhear a network of white mothers collectively bemoaning the inclusion of slavery in their children's early education. They nod in agreement that their children's innocence has been sacrificed far too early, that the school curriculum has interrupted the simplicity and joy of their youths. One mother asserts that the curricular lessons on enslavement have taught her child to *notice race for the first time.* Another responds in solidarity: *Why can't they wait until the kids are ready for it?*

Listening in, I envision myself as a curious anthropologist. In fact, I am nothing more or less than a seething eavesdropper. The vast majority of the Black and Brown students have been bused away with the ring of the bell, and the after-school population has become, once again, a mirror of its affluent neighborhood. The schoolyard is awash in whiteness. If indeed their children were as innocent and oblivious as they imagine, it is an oblivion of innocence that belongs to white children alone. Some children have the privilege of their innocence, while others learn their exclusions from both history and everyday experience. Everyone knows their place here.

Not only do I wish to abolish the cultivation of innocence but I wish for every child to learn the history of race and racism from below—from the position not of white leaders but from those who were brutalized under their leadership. I desire an infinitely more nuanced version of this history, an education that builds into evermore complex critical analyses of genocide, the reservation system, the Middle Passage, lynching, the politics of immigration, the internment camps, and the state tactics of minority divide and conquer. I want to hold you firmly and lovingly as you wade through the violence of these ever-present pasts. I yearn for an education made for life and living that sets off from the basic premise that there is a vital relation between the subjugation of peoples and the unrelenting destruction of our planet. An education that teaches against rather than for the neocolonial world order we have inherited. One through which, in the spirit of the We Will Remember Survival School, we are trained in the ancient ways of dwelling with our surroundings. Where we are taught law and justice from the vantage points of those it excludes, and guided to fight within and against the current legal and political systems through which destruction and disparity are made to flourish.

For many, this desire makes me the worst kind of mother: a radical, a killjoy, a thief. But I am not so different from these other mothers insofar as our most basic and bodily desires are to protect our children. The difference lies in how we conceive a politics of protection. To shield you from the violence of our ways of life is both an inherited logic and a catastrophic error, for you will not know how to change the world if you do not understand how it came to be this way. And you will not be able to envision your future— any future—without studying the traces of those who have endured and survived the brutalities of the past and present.

I am turning over questions I cannot yet answer: Against political and corporate systems that are plunging us full speed toward total ecological destruction, what will ultimately make our bodies gather and surge against them? Will we physically revolt against these systems, using our collective might to raze them to the ground? Or will we find another way to exercise our willful bodies in resistance? Can we withdraw ourselves en masse, bodies and minds, refusing to feed a system that thrives on our habits and labor, our lifestyles, our instilled consumptive desires?

Marx once predicted that the bourgeoisie would never be the source of a class revolution because they had too much to lose. They would cling to their property and the forms of individual freedom they held so dear. History has shown that few of us who benefit from the order of things are willing to compromise what we have for the good of the whole. If a class revolution was to come, Marx foresaw, it would have to come from the proletariat, the underclasses who had little to lose. Who in having little to lose would have the impetus to change the course of history. The revolution, in other words, was not going to come from people like me.

But shouldn't the immediate threat of human extinction trump the Marxist formulation of class revolution? Shouldn't knowing that extinctions are everywhere underway lead us to demolish the effacing forces that produce it? Regardless of class status, shouldn't the very fact of being your mother mean I am already sharpening my knives, fighting tooth and nail for our lives?

In *Lose Your Mother,* Saidiya Hartman chronicles her journey to the African "motherland," a journey that turns out to be less a homecoming than a series of discomforting estrangements. Hartman's journey provokes us to consider the critically incomplete and sometimes even false stories of our pasts, urging us to think otherwise about our inheritances. *Every generation confronts the task of choosing its past,* she writes. *Inheritances are chosen as much as they are passed on.* I think of you each time I read these words, think of all we know about our history and all that has been omitted, think of what you will choose from the past in pursuit of a future we might yet survive. I think also of the role of the mother—and of *losing* her—in the political act of culling from history and discarding what does not serve you. For as unabashedly attached as we are, I accept that you will need to loosen our bond as you make your own way in the world. I am not squeamish about this developmental loosening; I know that we must lose our mothers, often only later (and in a perverse twist) to become them in ways we may not be able to predict or appreciate.

It is less the inevitability of our break than it is the shape and force of it that haunts me. I know it is not just *me* you will need to break from, but the entire way of life that I represent. However liberally filled with reused plastic bags, farmers market purchases, and composting practices, this form of life is ushering us, and everyone else, toward the end of the world. More than any other time in history, what you choose from the past will need to be meticulously studied and selected. You will need to read beyond the official archives with a keen understanding that resistance, collective action, and stories of survival against all odds have been discarded by the grand narratives of history. You will need to cull carefully from the intimate and political pasts that have shaped your life, and you will need to draw respectfully from other histories of subjugation that are not yours but have had no less a hand in shaping you. You will need to discover and learn from these fragments, from ancient stories and lost practices, from the hints and traces of lives lived otherwise, from forms of resistance already underway that are not yet perceptible to you.

If, following Hartman, inheritances are as much chosen as they are passed on, I feel urgently compelled to offer myself to you in all my complicity and failure, inviting you to pick and choose from your maternal history what is important for you in the service of ongoing human life. What you will discover is a history of insufficiencies, of nearly unbelievable forms of denial, of living much more with than against the violently consumptive status quo. I hope that in sifting through my past, you might also stumble on obscured moments that lead you nearer to an elsewhere. Losing me, my way of life, is unquestionably a requisite to survival and futurity. Yet I hope with every thread of my being that this world-altering shift can become a form of breaking that does not sever us entirely, or wrench us into mutual unbelonging. My most intimate desire is that you find a way to break *with* me rather than to break *from* me. A desire in which the necessity of our breaking does not so much leave me behind in your struggle to survive as it invites me in and calls me to blaze alongside you. I yearn for our imminent break to be not an end, but an act of profound and collective renewal. In these early years of your life, I whisper to you a mantra in your sleep with the passionate hope that it will embolden you: *Break with me, break with me, break with me.*

I have moved beyond the initial impulse to apologize to you for planetary crisis. I offer less an apology than a wish for an *us* that is not yet *us;* an *us* who will teach and learn together what I have not been bold, desperate, or visionary enough to accomplish. An *us* that is joined not through biological or habitual belonging, not even through our mutual love, but through a passionate will to make life enduringly livable. In other words, an *us* that is willing to put our whole selves on the line, to abandon what we are and the world we have inherited in an unflinching effort to change the whole of it.

I write to you in the near aftermath of an emergency neurosurgery, the second and twinned body trauma I have sustained in your lifetime, and the first you will consciously remember. I am acutely aware that this bodily break and its painstakingly slow aftermath will leave an imprint on you that will endure. More than any other, this elongated moment in our lives feels like a memory being made and congealed. The memory of your mother losing her stoicism, becoming desperate and fearful, and eventually warping under pain and debility. The memory of your mother losing her capacity to mother you.

The discs between my vertebrae have begun to explode, making it appear to medical professionals as though my body is being subjected to high-impact collisions. *Have you been in an accident?* they ask each time. *Did something happen to you?* The questions leave me feeling strangely guilty. Medically speaking, there seems to be no point of origin to these breaks, no precise moment where they can be made logical. My body is a riddle, a mystery, fatefully unique. The specialists marvel at and treat each break, yet none of them seems particularly interested in playing the part of the sleuth who seeks out the source of the recurring traumas. I don't fault them at all. They have so many other desperate bodies to repair, and there is no guarantee that tracking backward toward an origin will change future outcomes. They are trained to treat the body as it is now, not to imagine it as it once was.

But there is in fact an origin story to these bodily breaks, one I have come to know as true, even if it remains unconfirmed from a medical perspective. It is a story every intimate person in my life knows well, both from listening to my historical recounting and from observing the strange, unwieldy shape of my right foot, a bulbous monument to a life-altering event. As a girl of thirteen I was, like many others, passionate about horses. I found myself one day riding an enormous chestnut stallion around an indoor arena. The stallion was passing through town, being hauled around by his owner so prospective buyers could take a look. Even then, I despised the notion of ownership, of buying and selling life, and in equal measures I felt achingly sorry for him and awed by his beauty. It was winter in Manitoba, and the weather had become unseasonably warm for a few days just before freezing up again. Through an act of unfortunate neglect, someone had left the pulley door open the previous day, allowing melting snow into the arena, which froze into sheer ice overnight just under the surface of the footing. The stallion was cantering around the arena, gaining confidence with me, when he suddenly slipped and came crashing down on his right side. His hulking body landed squarely on my leg, crushing me under the weight of thousands of pounds. He then sprang up, stunned but unwounded, and trotted away.

I was lifted onto a horse blanket and edged into a tiny back bench of a truck, which sped its way toward the city. *Is he okay?* I kept asking in desperation. *He's fine!* someone said from the front seat. *You buffered his fall!* We were pulled over by highway police for speeding, then escorted with sirens through the city to the emergency room up the street from our house. My mother was waiting at the hospital when we arrived. She held my hand while they cut off my clothes. I lost myself to pain as my foot, cut free from the riding boot, swelled into inhuman shape and size, then I quickly succumbed to a morphine haze from which I felt grateful to have my mother's full focus, her unmistakable concern a special sign of her love.

The head of orthopedic surgery was on vacation, so I was seen instead by a younger surgeon. Whereas the older man would not have hesitated to cut me open, the junior surgeon advocated for a less interventionist approach. Because the bones of the foot and leg were so badly crushed, he explained, the surgery would be an exhaustive jigsaw puzzle of hardware in a shattered landscape. Rather than cut me open and tackle the impossible damage, he wanted to take the unconventional approach, immobilizing me to see how my broken body might work to heal itself. *Young bodies can heal in amazing ways,* he said. *In this kind of crisis, we often do more damage than good with reconstructive interventions.* Then he took my mother aside and explained that the injuries were severe enough that with or without surgery, I might never properly use the leg again. He admitted me to the children's ward, where I lived immobilized for weeks in a narcotic ease that stripped away any pubescent capacity I had to navigate the weight of what had befallen me. The leg was too swollen to be casted, so it remained raised and steadied in a contraption at the end of the bed. By day, I kept perfectly still. But at night, when I dreamed of riding or running, of life as it was before, my leg would twitch involuntarily, and I would wake to my own piercing screams.

Once the swelling began to subside, my foot and leg were gathered and bound in a huge, imposing cast. Because my mother was trained as a nurse, I was eventually permitted to transfer home. I had almost no mobility, so I lived in our TV room on the foldout sofa bed because it was nearest to the bathroom. Eventually, I graduated from full bed rest to a wheelchair, returning to eighth grade almost fully dependent on the aid of my wayward teen counterparts to roll me from class to class. The time thereafter was an eternity of crutches, followed by years of walking with an unmistakable limp. I dragged my right leg with me, launching my hip forward by the force of my left side while the right foot trailed clumsily along. The sole of my orthopedic shoe left skid marks behind me like a junior high trail to nowhere.

The foot eventually healed by wildly overcorrecting itself, my body creating an elaborate new geography of calcification, becoming newly monstrous in shape and size. So keen to recover from the breaks, it emerged as much more than its former self, making abundantly clear that it was never going back. From the top of the foot wrapping all the way around the inside of the arch, the newly formed structure protruded like a mountainous landscape. A couple of years after the accident, I underwent an extremely painful orthopedic surgery to shave down the overcalcified bone, forming it into something more resembling a foot. It was a practical surgery, less cosmetic than aimed at reshaping the appendage into something that might once again fit into a standard shoe. I wonder now if this choice was a kind of injustice—to enter the scene of the break surgically, stripping away so much of what my body had made for itself in service of its healing.

Decades later, as the neurosurgeon examines the scans of my spine and asks whether I have been in an accident, the question arises as a temporal trick. The answer is a short no and a long yes. The medical specialists cannot confirm whether the old equestrian break is the root cause of the more recent and mysterious spinal ones, though after two unbelievable neurosurgeries in the last several years, we all finally recognize the clear and simple fact that all the breaks have occurred on the right side of my body. For many months after this last surgery, the lack of medical confirmation haunted me. I wanted someone with authority to prove this connection for me, to remove any mystery. Yet over time, the absence of medical evidence ceases to deter me from knowing and feeling this connection as a bodily truth, from acknowledging that the weakness of my right leg and foot have caused an accrual of stress and intense impact on my spine over time. That original break will continue to emerge in my body, as a life that cannot help but live out its afterlives.

I began to write this letter in autumn, in the weeks building to the release of a book I had written that sought to craft an archive of the body. There, I wanted to gather the material and affective aspects of the body we are trained to disavow, and in so doing, to re-member the body as an entity that is always sloughing, leaking, absorbing, discarding, and remaking itself in relation with an outside world. I wrote the book after my first neurosurgery, an event I described in detail to meditate otherwise on the body, ruminating over how pain had devoured the being I thought I was and revealed something else. In finishing the manuscript, I felt entirely done with the body and had no intention of returning to it in future writing. I was relieved to set the body aside, turning my attention to maternal matters, which I realize now is so strikingly absurd.

The week the archive book was released, I was in Los Angeles for a series of book events. I had been suffering for months from hauntingly similar symptoms to those that preceded my first neurosurgery, but had been assured by medical professionals that my problems were of a muscular nature, and my worries simply the post-traumatic effects of that past experience. In Los Angeles, I began to feel a deep nausea in my core, like car sickness that would not abate. On the day of the release, I did a recorded interview with the hosts of the *Los Angeles Review of Books Radio Hour*, where we had a lively discussion about body archives and laughed over some of the unseemly aspects of the book. I found myself historicizing my surgery as a thing of the past, even while I perched on the edge of my chair to find a comfortable position against oncoming pain, and even while I promoted a book that insisted on vulnerability as a necessary, enduring form of politics.

When I awoke the next day to travel home to the East Coast, back to you, I had lost feeling and strength in my right leg from my knee through my foot. I limped through airports and arrived home to acknowledge that my leg was losing an alarming amount of strength. By the end of my first week home, I had become a danger to myself. Walking our eight-pound terrier around the block, I fell repeatedly, flat out on the ground, just trying to take the next step. Three weeks after the book's release, after a desperate struggle to schedule an MRI during the Thanksgiving holiday season and an all-out war with my insurance company, which initially

refused to approve the procedure, I was back in the operating room undergoing another emergency surgery. The
neurosurgeon called me in immediately and declared that
I had no choice but to undergo another surgery. Unable
to conceal his concern over my palpable loss of mobility,
he told me unflinchingly that he could not be sure how
much strength would return to the leg. We had twenty-
four hours to prepare for the surgery.

I had lived out the years following my first neurosurgery as
one who had undergone something singular and unrepeat-
able. My neurosurgeon, astounded at the time by the mass
that had ruptured and crushed my spinal nerves, named
my injury *a fluke*. It was, we came to believe, something
that happens to a body without rhyme or reason, a moment
when a body inexplicably breaks. *Fluke* became a mantra for
moving forward, a response—as public as it was private—
that covered over the strange shame of being a body that
had fallen apart. This despite an embrace of vulnerability
that was at the heart of my ethics and politics, of virtually
everything I wrote and professed. I embraced others in vulnerability almost instinctively, yet I had no capacity to
abide my own emotional or physical precarity. I have been
trained across my life to remain composed, to stay stoic
even while I am falling apart. It has always felt disgraceful
to come undone, whether physically or emotionally, even
while I thrive on guiding others through their anguish. I was
ashamed of what had befallen me and took on a perverse
sense of blame for my body's unexplained break. When the
surgeon declared my rupture a *fluke*, I became wholeheartedly attached to the idea of myself as someone who had made
it through a strange and inexplicable event. A story to tell

from the future, even with a kind of narrative pleasure as it receded into the past. A history that had little bearing on the present, until it repeated.

Five years later, as we awaited a diagnosis that would swiftly force us to abandon the narrative of the fluke, I turned to you. I needed to brace us both for the imminent event and its long, uncertain aftermath, and to account for why I had been crying so much over the past weeks and months, by explaining the trauma of my first neurosurgery. I told you how I had been unable to care for you during that time of your infancy, how brutal it had been for us both when we were separated for the first time in an effort to heal me. *When I was admitted to the hospital, we had never spent any time apart. Our bodies were still tethered,* I said. As I spoke, I became palpably aware that I was bracing myself as much as I was trying to prepare you, that something in my breaking body was making the difference between a discrete *you* and *me* harder to parse.

You told me you knew the story well, gently reminding me that my narrative offering was also a repetition, sealed as part of our family lore. Then, with all the promise you held in your body, you said, *It will be so different this time, Amma, because I'm grown up now, and we don't have to be separated. I can help you heal.* I was struck by the sentiment, which seemed to understand that while I was being pulled back into the past, you needed to stretch yourself forward into a future, when you would have the capacity to care for me. I felt in that moment that we were time travelers, stitching ourselves through the ether so one of us was always holding the other from an elsewhere. In the breaking, it seemed that we were coming closer together, our bodies moving toward each other, both holding the crisis as one.

In the hospital after the surgery, your eyes were moon-wide as you drew back the curtain and tiptoed quietly toward me. For the first time in your life, you were unsure how to approach the body you love more than any other. You stood beside my bed and reached for my hand, folding it into yours before bending to kiss it quickly and softly. I could not discern whether this was a royal gesture or a romantic one; perhaps it was both. You fed me spoonful after spoonful of yogurt and cafeteria soup, brushed your fingertips across my face, then quietly inched around the post-op ward to see if there were any other patients in need of your care. When you left, I felt joyful, high on narcotics and flooded with relief. I opened my email to find the *Los Angeles Review of Books* interview had just aired, and listened eerily to my voice on the radio talking about bodies coming undone and being made anew in contact with other bodies in the world.

For months after the surgery, you were gentle and attentive, quick to apologize when you forgot my wound, when you pulled or pounced too hard on my body, causing me to wince or cry. You observed me almost anthropologically—as though my most intimate body had become a stranger to you, a stranger you knew molecularly, whom you could not turn away from. Less than a year later, it is easy to remember the surgical time as a series of jarring interruptions in our lives: An interruption to my capacity to care for you. An interruption to my fraudulent performance as a self that had broken and reemerged steadfastly whole again. An interruption to the letter I was beginning to write to you that had little at all to do with the body. What we are learning in the long thereafter is that interruptions are occasions for reorientation, for producing necessary and new ways of living. We are beginning to lean into the breaks because we must, because in this requisite shift we can sense profound potential to become a more promising form of our collective selves.

When you surfaced from my body, the midwife placed you on my skin. I searched your body as a new landscape, looking for a familiar place to begin. I was in awe of you as a tiny living thing, and felt there to be something unbelievable about our relation. I mean this quite literally; it was *hard to believe* we belonged to one another, that a series of bodily acts had led to your existence, and that you were suddenly my child and I your mother. I did not feel like a mother, which is to say I did not feel toward you what I had been told mothers felt toward their offspring. I did not recognize you or know you already. I did, however, feel acutely interested in you, though I am not sure that this interest could be called love.

My love for you developed over the early months of your life unfolding. I studied you and watched you study me, two intimate aliens learning each other and discovering ourselves otherwise. I felt myself being slowly turned outward, pulled through like a stitch.

During night feedings in the early months after your birth, I sat beside the window in an ugly rocking chair that had been sent as a maternity gift by way of a big-box store. I strongly disliked the chair, both aesthetically and practically, and decried the space it took up in the apartment. I used it because it seemed requisitely maternal. One night, as we rocked and nursed in the unpalatable chair, I was suddenly overcome by a piercing feeling in my gut. Stricken by pain, I began to sob. Your father came stumbling into the room in a dazed panic and kneeled beside us. *Are you okay?* he asked, reaching for us both. Your mouth dropped lazily off my nipple as you fell into deep sleep. I drew in my breath, then exhaled slowly in an attempt to garner my own stability. *I just realized that to lose her would ruin me,* I said, remembering that love is not simply a psychic risk but an unabashedly bodily one.

Once, in the course of a conversation about beginnings and ends, you said something so striking to me: *There's always an afterward, except when you are dead.* You were four, maybe five, and had felt death in proximity through the sudden passing of my father, then our beloved cat, followed by your paternal grandmother. Riffing on your formulation, we mused over this time after death. I suggested death itself might be a crucial kind of afterward. *The time after death may well be the most generative of all afterwards,* I said, *because during that time, you become earth, no longer playing out the fantasy of being other to this world. As a countless host of organisms, you become unabashedly ecological.* We daydreamed for a while about what it might be like to grow into another kind of living being. *Maybe when we die, we'll both grow together and become a tree,* you suggested. We stretched our bodies long across my bed and thought about the world as a regenerative ecosystem, and about the strange fiction of beginnings and ends that so often inhibits the full flourishing of our immediately unfolding lives.

You have grown up with the term *best friends* to describe the relation between your parents, though this term is simply a stand-in for one that has not yet been invented. Nathan and I are in fact infinitely more than friends. We are queer collaborators who adore each other and who are raising you collectively, living our lives adjacently as we play with what constitutes family. For now, that your parents are best friends as opposed to a romantic couple does not strike you as the least bit odd, though from time to time you like to feign worry that we might one day *break apart*, playing out the narrative of a divorce drama with a wink and nod to our curiously unflappable relationship.

I met Nathan in 2003 when I moved to the United States to begin graduate school, though it took five more years before we sealed our friendship. He likes to joke that I didn't know who he was for those first years, which holds some degree of truth because he was part of a sea of theoretically driven white boys whom I tended to find estranging. Years into our graduate educations, we had a chance encounter over the winter holidays in the office space shared by graduate students. We had both chosen to avoid the emotional perils of traveling home, and we each had assumed we would find ourselves alone on campus. A true pedagogue in the making, Nathan stumbled into the office carrying an enormous stack of photocopies, clearly overpreparing for a course he would be teaching in spring semester. While we chatted, he held the coveted photocopies in precarious balance. I was endeared by how preciously he treated his unruly cargo, a wealth of critical material that might change the world.

At the time, I was in deep worry over an impending endoscopy to diagnose my recurring stomach pain. I knew that the combination of induced vomiting to manage stress and excessive caffeine consumption was the root of my problem, but the pain had intensified, and I worried I had crossed a threshold and caused internal damage. I was sitting at a public computer (in the days before I had my own laptop), googling the doctor who was scheduled to do the procedure. Nathan asked what I was up to, and rather than minimize or shut down the screen, I shared my endoscopic fears and invited him into my search. We laughed at the online image of the doctor who wore his hair in a thinning white comb-over, bantering about whether this style choice made us trust his professional prowess more or less. I felt oddly at ease, filled with an unexpected warmth that seemed to both emanate from within my body and fuel me from the outside. It would take months before I shared with him my bulimic secret, and years more for him to learn all my other wayward habits, but as all were revealed, I felt a total absence of pathological shame, no compulsion at all to be otherwise.

We were full tilt after that happenstance meeting. Every week after our Tuesday afternoon spring semester seminar, we sat at the happy hour sushi bar in Uptown Minneapolis and breathlessly indulged topics as far flung as Gayatri Spivak's particular use of the word *we,* the global climate crisis, and the unusually large, elfin shape of Nathan's ears.

We were inexhaustible in our capacities to reach for each other. To formally inaugurate our friendship, we pooled our money to purchase a Jack LaLanne juicer, an item we each desired but couldn't individually afford. Juicing was a nefarious capitalist fad of the time, and we became convinced that the incredibly wasteful dietary regime was key to our health and longevity. Since most of our time was spent in dusty libraries and smoky coffee shops where we ignored our bodies to feed our minds, juicing seemed a gateway to a healthier life. Our friends couldn't resist joking about our practice of "juicing together," an unsubtle euphemism for sex. We laughed along, knowing something else was afoot, even if we couldn't quite grasp the feeling and form of our strange intimacy—how it held us differently in time and space, the way it never let us go.

We coined the term *friends-in-love* to describe our relation while smoking pot and sipping juice at my old Formica table. I had just returned from a trip to the Bay Area, where a would-be fling in wine country had gone woefully awry. Having nowhere else to go, I crashed in Berkeley with friends, a queer couple with a penchant for rescue. We spent the evening before I flew home evaluating my flailing romantic life. My friends invited me to write a list of five characteristics I could not do without in a future partner, which I scrawled on a piece of scrap paper that remains to this day in the drawer of my bedside table. I was embarrassed by performing this task, which seemed both a practical undertaking aimed at offering me personal clarity and a witchy conjuring to manifest my ideal person. The next day, fresh off my flight, as I lumbered down Franklin Avenue on the number 2 bus, I passed Nathan's street and felt an overwhelming sense of arrival. I considered the feeling for days, wondering over a bonded connection that was neither conventionally romantic nor simply amicable. A week later at the Formica table, giddy and stoned, I gathered the courage to present Nathan with my *friends-in-love* formulation. He smiled elatedly—accepting wholeheartedly what was, in retrospect, a queer proposal.

We were intimate accomplices, misfits bunking collectively in my minuscule apartment. We studied together, learning in constant communion. Nathan seemed to live on my old orange sofa, flat on his back with a novel or book of philosophy in hand, while my once-feral cat, Cassie, slept on his belly. He wouldn't move for anything if she was content, even though she made a practice of attacking him in unanticipated intervals to ensure he knew his place among us—a newcomer, a man. He was and remains the gentlest person I have ever known, and the first relationship of any kind in my life—whether filial, friendly, or romantic—that grew through a total lack of judgement or possessive feeling. Nothing about me deterred him or made him bristle. He approached me as he did his most coveted works of literature, with meticulous care and textual precision, with repetition, reading me over and over again with a lasting patience, interpreting my gaps and fissures not as failures but as opportunities for sense-making. It is harder from this vantage point to say what he has gained through our queer solidarity, but I know he finds in me an unflappable kinship we never knew we could desire for ourselves.

Amid our leap into late-onset adulthood, we felt the hailing of normativity, the strong sense that we should make our relationship legible for the world. We merged into a couple form, following a straight path because we didn't yet have the drive to blaze another trail. When I finished my PhD and got an assistant professor job in Virginia, we packed up our graduate student lives and headed southeast in a beat-up old Honda Civic. We lived out our heterosexual union, happily nesting for the long haul, living a deeply affectionate though largely nonsexual life. More often than not, we treated sexuality with humor. Nathan teased me about my unabashed attraction to butches, a fact I had always thought was an imperceptible desire. In turn, I joked that in our awkward sex, Nathan seemed to be keeping full-throttled anxiety attacks at bay, suffering his way through an act he would have much preferred to avoid. I referred to Nathan as *monastic,* which I still think best describes his style of being. This was years before *asexual* found its way into a public vocabulary, so we had little language for someone who simply preferred not to engage in sexual contact with others. His library and his collection of records have always been his love objects of choice, so much so that he has written evocatively about the sensuality of those particular relations. I was still at a remove from using *queer* to describe myself, not because I had any hesitation about queer sexualities, but because I was uneasy about laying claim to preexisting identity categories.

In the couple form, we would lapse from time to time into a pathological approach to our sex life, feeding a mutual worry that our scant and uneasy sexual contact constituted a lack between us. At a critical juncture of our relationship, we descended into a corrective frenzy and sought medical advice for Nathan's muted sex drive. He underwent testing

that concluded he had abnormally low levels of testoster-
one and was prescribed injections to restore him into the
proper fold of normative masculinity. Nathan was unfalter-
ing in response to the medical prescription, unequivocally
declaring *I am who I am and I hold the politics I hold precisely
because I fall beyond the capture of normativity.* He refused
to be delivered into corrective masculinity, or to aspire
anymore to an other-oriented sexual drive. It was such a
simple act, to commit without pause to accepting himself
exactly as he was; I felt astonished by the gesture, so mundane as to be spectacular.

Rather than break from each other at this crucial point, we
broke instead from traditional ideas about what constitutes
love and family. I followed Nathan's commitment to simple
gestures, allowing us to live our lives exactly as we were,
and in so doing to change the entire feel of it. Disengaging
from a sexual fantasy of lasting love, we offered each other
instead an enduring home, the safest place to falter and
thrive. A place, as psychic as it is spatial, in which to break
and to heal, to come apart when we must, then to mend
into new alignments. We became what we already were:
friends who make family together, who raise a wild little
human and offer sanctuary to stray animals, who collabo-
rate intellectually, who make meals together and bandage
each other's wounds. Friends who, in breaking from con-
vention, have become unbreakable.

In fullest embrace of our queer alliance, we spent time
after your birth dreaming up antinormative styles of being

together. Freed from the grip of heteronormative relationality, we sought out a life that felt more queerly capacious.
We were three humans now rather than two, so there
was no fantasy of a return to what we once were. Because
Nathan and I are academics, we approached this vision
theoretically, trying to think our way into our new lives.
In actuality, we were already steeped in the life we were
trying to invent theoretically, already living the life we
were attempting to conjure. We made minor adjustments
to our everyday living arrangements, playing with architectural spaces designed for the heterosexual nuclear family. A few months before, we had put in a lowball offer on a
small house we magically ended up landing. We converted
our master bedroom into an all-purpose bedroom-office
space simply by moving furniture around, transforming
it into something that felt like an oddly comforting
return to college life. In turn, we adapted the small study
down the hall into a second bedroom-office, creating two
autonomous dwelling spaces. Periodically, we swapped our
bedroom-offices, defamiliarizing and refamiliarizing ourselves within the rooms that held us. Initially, I slept in
the front bedroom with the big bed, where I fell asleep
nursing you every night. But come spring, when the sugar
maple in the backyard came into foliage and the birds
were all song and moxie, I wanted to look out a window
while I wrote, so we switched rooms for the sake of crea-
tive inspiration.

Through our meditations on queer cohabitation, we became
besotted by the notion of adjacency—of living contigu-
ously, consciously alongside others, in proximities beyond
the bounds of normative relationality. We embraced what

we called *adjacent living,* a style of dwelling together in which we lived side by side as cocreators who envisioned together, read each other tirelessly, and raised you in shared wonderment. As a queer duo inhabiting our lives differently together, we cultivated our boundless friendship, learning through the long days of your earliest childhood that even if the form of us could not be made easily legible to an outside world, it could be fully lived. In the first years of this practice, we wrestled with whether to call our experiment an act of *living together apart,* or of *living apart together.* By now, we are less preoccupied with capturing the theoretical form of our queer family than we are with existing in the felt rhythms of our lives unfolding.

We daydreamed for a few years about coauthoring an essay called "Queer Architectures," a shared reflection on how relationships develop within and against the architectural shapes that house us. Architecture anticipates ways of living in the spaces we rent or buy, presumes conventions of living that are literally built into the structures we dwell in. Unless you own property and have some degree of wealth, you can't really change the shape of it; you simply find ways to live in the spaces you can afford, in the shapes that are already preconfigured and set in stone. By pure necessity or needful desire, some of us make a craft of playing within these fields, subverting architectural presumptions by living in and against them otherwise. Nathan and I have lived together now for much of what constitutes our adult lives, and so our history of architecture now spans five collective living spaces: one tiny studio apartment, two two-bedroom rentals, a single-family house we bought as a couple, and a duplex we now own as a queer collective.

We dwelled easily in rental spaces, living on top of each other as we sought advanced degrees and edged our way toward upward mobility. We were accustomed to the struggle to pay our monthly bills, happy to make our lives more afford- able by sharing rental space with each other as we studied Marxist theory, decrying ownership as the ascending slip into an antirevolutionary bourgeois life. Once we ourselves had "arrived," we felt as uneasy about property ownership as we had begun to feel about paying outrageous rental costs into someone else's mortgage. I had been taking daily walks with you nestled in a sling over my shoulder, and I kept unconsciously finding my way to the beautiful little brick house on Allen Avenue that seemed to be languishing on the real estate market. When we finally contacted an agent to let us see the house, the languishing made immediate sense. It was occupied by a pair of pack-rat lesbians who loved thick, dark adornment: huge overstuffed black leather sofas, an excess of furniture, and deep-red velvet curtains blocking out any natural light, all combined to give the small house the feel of a funeral parlor.

I possess few talents, but one is a capacity to envision space as a blank slate, my mind imaginatively working to clear away all the clutter, to let in the sunlight, to see a sparse clean otherworld in the one bearing down in real time. Nathan took some convincing as I walked him through the house a second time and invoked, room by room, another spatial and affective scene. The lesbian couple had already bought a suburban home with multiple bathrooms, plenty of garage space for their three cars, and ample room for their leather sofas. One of them, I learned later through our written correspondence, had been married to a man for twenty-five years and had had two children, who were now grown, before finding her best love. Somehow, this knowledge made their suburban dreams feel less egregious to me. In any case, they were relieved to sign the house over to us, to begin another kind of life together.

The house on Allen was what the world around us called *a perfect starter home*. This formulation irritated me in its presumption that of course we were embarking on a pre-destined path that would obviously and increasingly lead us to wanting and needing more: more babies, more yard, more furniture, more storage space for an endless amassing of useless things. In its very articulation *starter home* also willfully discarded the homes we had lived in before, those intimate dwelling spaces we never possessed but that were no less intimate to our lives, our histories. To boot, the phrase was a blatant repetition of what my mentors and colleagues had recently echoed about my newly landed academic position—*a perfect starter job*—as though the liberal arts college that had employed me was a mere stepping stone to bigger, better places. We found ourselves in an economy of willful upward mobility, where even the lefty radicals who trained us were endlessly scrambling for more. Where there was a linear path of action and desire, beyond which anything else appeared as failure.

In fact, the purchase of our *starter home* turned out to be more of a hetero endgame, the place where we veered off the pre-scribed path and consciously embarked on the cooperative work of making another style of family life. Like all modest single-family homes, the architecture of the Allen house presumed a small nuclear family, and we struggled over our three years there to fit easily within its frame. A master bedroom in the front was spatially arranged for two reproductive parents, while a skinny hallway led those parents to the smaller bedrooms of two little offspring. One room seemed perfectly designed for a crib, the other for a growing child. And when the second baby was big enough, the start was over, and it was time to move to the next dwelling space. I didn't want more of anything. And I certainly didn't want to outgrow the space by means of further object purchases or acts of human reproduction. A modern capitalist feel seemed to have seeped into its foundations, the expectations of a clamoring reproductive family filling the space, then making its way toward a bourgeois elsewhere. It didn't take long before its nuclear family feeling and the starter home expectations that had seeped into its pores began to feel suffocating.

History tells me that the architect who designed the Allen house was not, in fact, thinking of a starter life that would lead to a more expansive suburban American dream house. The house was designed and built long ago for a cookie-cutter middle-class family who would likely never move, for people who would abide in the house until the eventualities of sickness or death turned it over to a new set of lives. A kitchen renovation gave it a modern feel, and a small unheated addition off the back of the kitchen led onto a backyard deck. The house had been occasionally modified over time, but much remained as it always was. In the basement, a Jim Crow toilet stood bare and exposed against the southeast perimeter wall, reminding us both of the political history of the space, and the ways the house would never outgrow its haunting origins. In its exposed obscurity—out in the open without the dignity of walls, yet hidden below ground—the toilet was a brutal legacy, an architectural trace of racial servitude that persisted over time as a sobering monument.

We played with space in that old house, changing nothing structural but the ways our bodies lived in it. No matter what moves we made, what shapes we tried to assume therein, it seemed to summon an unwanted path for our lives. We dreamed for a while about making architectural shifts, moving its walls and perimeters not so much to make more space but to make more self-contained spaces. Our aim was to give ourselves little pods within the home, spaces to think and feel and write in isolation, thereby making the whole space feel more psychically capacious. My stepfather, an Italian architect with incredible imaginative scope for shapes and spaces, offered us his services in dreaming up new possibilities. He was at work on two major building projects: one, a conversion of a Winnipeg curling rink into a community space for autistic folks, and the other, a nursing station on an Indigenous reservation in northern Manitoba. In both projects, he understood his work to be an act of skillful immersion into the everyday practices and worldviews of the communities he served. I admired his capacity to envision and create spaces for collectives so different from him, his desire to make alter-architectures possible for those whose lives are shaped through otherworldly attunements. Even while the particular valences of our queer family life may not have made perfect sense to my parents, who were quite content with our more recognizable union, I knew from his professional commitments and his deep love of us that he desired to make us feel more at home.

We FaceTimed with him one night after we put you to bed and smoked a little pot for added inspiration. When we started to describe our fanciful renovation ideas, my step-father stopped us in our tracks. *Don't tell me what you want the house to look like,* he said. *Tell me how you want to feel in it, what kind of life you want to live there.*

In a slightly stoned reverie, we detailed our theory of adjacency for him while we watched him nod and scrawl rough designs on a paper that lay just out of view. With a nursing child and a body that had been given over to another, I desired a door I could slide closed, a contained space (a room of one's own, come to think of it) where I could live for a day, or two, or three with warm light on my skin, my thoughts feeling their way into being. Nathan's desires for endless reading days, and his propensity for excessively loud doom metal and nineties emo, painted a very different picture of a dark, subterranean life, a soundproof den where witchy things could manifest unabated. We wanted shared meals, rambling kitchen time, family spaces where we would wear out the rugs with our endless gatherings. When my stepdad raised his sketches, I started to cry with the pleasure and possibilities of building another world right where we lived. But when we walked up the street to meet a local architect we hoped might bring the sketches to life, we quickly realized we lacked the monumental amounts of disposable income it would take to manifest those particular dreams.

The Allen house accrued some value in a skyrocketing housing market, I got tenure at the university where I worked, and we sold the house, taking a financial and emotional leap into a new form of adjacent living. It's no coincidence that we ended up in a duplex, a space designed for transient renters, occupants who would move in and out of the split building, whose lives were not, or not yet, on the road to indebted property possession and the starter life. The space presumed no relation between the upstairs and downstairs occupants, simply two discrete units in which two sets of lives temporarily unfolded, some wealthy owner in the distance paying off his mortgage with the sweat of their rent. For us, the duplex held a different kind of potential, an opportunity to live our lives with the solitude we each yearned for and the adjacency we never stopped desiring. Together apart, apart together.

Nathan found the duplex while I was on a writing retreat in Brooklyn, so he toured the space alone, then called me immediately afterward with an unprecedented and breathless real estate certainty. We beelined to the duplex when I returned home, and while I quickly saw potential in the beleaguered old house, this time it was I who felt trepidation. The prospect of living the life we so desired was also fear inducing, perhaps for the simple reason that big changes produce anxiety, and I'm always busy keeping my already present anxiety at bay. Fear inducing also because I had come to rely on Nathan's immediate presence, the security of his body nearby over a decade of living in the closest proximities, through the profound intimacy of our four hands tending to your newborn body, and through my own debility and healing during that same time. We wandered through the slightly cavernous bottom unit where Nathan unquestionably belonged, then up the stairs, where an empty two-bedroom apartment filled with sunlight and trees in every window beckoned us home.

When we enter the creaky front gate, the concrete path that leads toward the house quickly splits in two, one path leading to Nathan's front door and the other to mine. The facade of the house suggests lives of total separation, though the back staircase has become a structural weave that holds us all together. Partly enclosed and partly exposed to the elements, the staircase is a witness to the always up-and-down traffic of our mingling bodies. Its steps hold us together, moving in one linear direction, then swerving around a quick corner and delivering us into the fold of family life. Your bedroom is upstairs with me, and contains a storehouse of experiments and jars holding the teeth you've shed, the whiskers and fur of animals we've loved and lost, an unexplained collection of old nail clippings, cicada exoskeletons, and a butterfly wing we found smashed into concrete. It's more of a workshop and laboratory than a bedroom, a place where your thinking increasingly takes flight without the guidance or stranglehold of your parents.

Our daily life in the duplex is structured by collective gathering—bustling through our morning rituals together, sharing our meals at the old farmhouse table downstairs, meeting upstairs after supper for bath time, when Nathan (for years now) pleads with you to dry your wet body as you race through rooms leaving a trail of puddles he can't tolerate. Then bedtime stories, when I study the tenor of Nathan's voice as you gather little objects in bed, playing aimlessly as you absorb the stories that are shaping your sense of the world. As a family, we are together more than any other I have known, more than I thought a family could want to be. If we so desire, we can close up the units and live in temporary solitude, though now that we have access to that potential, we discover we rarely need or claim it. We have made two discrete apartments into a single queer home. Two units that are also one; one home that is also more than itself.

We are not alone in our architectural play. We live among other animals and insects, some that are invited in as family members and others that are unabashedly unwelcome. A stray old terrier and two black kittens are especially beloved here, while others are ushered away, such as the rat that appeared in the basement last Christmas, and the gaggle of mice that swiftly took hold of the duplex over an especially cold winter. There is also the case of the sprickets who loom on the basement stairs to the laundry room, pouncing on us each time we need to clean our clothes. You used to love the sprickets and named each one (Peanut Butter, Teacup, Luigi, Butch . . .), until you grew up and they proliferated, becoming too many to name. As a family, we consider the ethics of this form of living, how some are invited in and loved, some tolerated, and others driven out.

Over the last decade of our lives in the American South, the architectures that have housed us are imprinted with histories of slavery and racialized servitude. How we move and feel throughout these houses, how we make them into homes, is informed and haunted by these brutal pasts. In the face and feeling of all this, we make home through questions, asking ourselves and each other who fits here, and why. Why do some bodies move through and around this space comfortably, while others are made to feel alien? What are the boundaries of the duplex, and where are its seams? How can this space become more than its bricks and boards? More than its racist history? More than a shield that conceals our private lives? More than a thing we have bought on loan? More than the privilege of financial investment? More than your economic inheritance? These questions keep us in our heads, in the realm of theory where the adults in our family feel most at home. You, on the other hand, have already begun to push theory to its limits, pressuring us to consider how our beliefs might become a living politics.

We are on the street, gazing at a sprawling red brick house. I am admiring the exterior architecture aloud, inviting you to wonder with me over the shapes within. There's a carriage house at the edge of the backyard, a loft space I envision as a writing den. I've always found this notion romantic, an artistic bourgeois fantasy of stumbling out your door through the flowers into a studio space where your work could unfold in quiet solitude. *You'd need an enormous family to fill this house. What would we do with all that space?* I ask rhetorically. Without missing a beat, you offer a quickly calculated response: *I have a perfect plan! We could move into a corner of the house on the second floor, and open up spaces in the house for homeless kids and their families. We could make separate rooms for each of the families, and a shared playroom for the kids that I could fill with my old toys. I could babysit the kids so the parents have time for themselves, and we could make huge pots of soup every day that would always be cooking on the stove for anyone who feels hungry. Can we do this? Can we please?* I adore this vision, in which our lives become oriented around service to others, rather than the queer crafting of space for our familial selves. I feel myself differently through your articulation, exposed by my limits but also filled with desire for your dream of a life I am not yet living. *I love this idea so much,* I say, curbing a swell of emotion. *You know, Amma, if we all shared the space upstairs in the duplex, we could open Nathan's apartment to people who needed it. We don't need a mansion to do this!* Although I know this conversation is spontaneous, it's delivered as though you've been plotting it for months now, preparing your pitch. You offer a clear layout for where the families would live and sleep in the duplex, which existing doors could be shut for their privacy, which rooms could be maintained for collective gathering and play. As far as I can see, there is no flaw in your plan. Nothing stands in our way aside from a point of contact where my conceptual willingness collides with my hesitation to transform the conditions of our lives for a larger whole. A tug-of-war in which my self-contained privilege pulls hard against the promises of your desired politics.

As soon as we shifted into the duplex, we set up my writing space in a room originally designed as a dining room. I got to work immediately on a short essay about Brazilian artist Néle Azevedo's *Minimum Monument,* an ephemeral public art project composed of hundreds of tiny human ice figures positioned in urban spaces. From the moment they are installed, the sculptures are already in thaw, already vanishing in contact with the atmosphere and under the viewer's gaze. Little humans disappearing before our eyes. Drip, drip, drip. The exhibit began as Azevedo's 2003 master's thesis, a project that sought to intervene in the dominant logic and form of the national monument. Against the heft of durable urban structures that remember "big" histories, these small perishable sculptures ask us to watch the disappearance of minor figures, ones whose lives do not play out grand historical gestures of the logics of conquest, exploitation, and unrelenting development. In this sense, they summon us to think and feel dynamically about forms of extinction and the forces that produce it.

Azevedo's exhibit hinges on time—on the temporal movement of individual and collective sculptural transformation from solid to liquid. If we wait long enough in observance, all signs of the exhibit will vanish as though nothing was ever there. It is no surprise that *Minimum Monument* has been received and celebrated as a commentary on global warming, as a sign of human extinction, the ways some bodies are disappearing faster than others, how the species as a whole will likely not survive the trajectories of global capitalism and the enduring histories that have given rise to it. Yet watching these figures as they vanish is also an experience of observing what is not entirely perceptible: the process of becoming vapor, of atmospheric reabsorption. In this sense, the exhibit pressures the very notion of disappearance, provoking us to consider what is beyond our capacities of perception, what falls outside of History. Azevedo's work reminds us that everything lost or stamped out by the force of History continues to exist in other earthly forms long after the brute fact of extinction.

I am not a scholar of the monument but a thinker compelled by those often-ignored or imperceptible historical traces that constitute our everyday lives. In the essay, I was making a case for why we should see a crucial relation between the artist's conception of the installation and its reception, between a critique of the historical monument and the threat of human extinction. Through its very inception, the grand historical monument indulges a fantasy of material and ideological stability; it comes into being through a belief that it will endure as a material object, and that the way we interpret the monument will carry over into the future. Both the grand historical monument and the machinations of extractive capitalism take the present as ideologically and materially stable, acting toward the present as a time of mastery, a time in which the logic of neocolonial capitalism will continue to dominate in a recognizably "progressive" future.

Wandering the new rooms of the duplex, you peer over my shoulder at my computer screen and asked with piqued interest about the images of the human ice figures. I tell you they are tiny sculptures made by a Brazilian artist. *But they just melt away? After she worked so hard to make them?* you ask. *Yes, love, they just melt away.*

We study the images, one after another, looking at how the sculptures melt at different rates depending on where they are situated in relation to the sun. *If we were seeing this in real time, our role would be to witness the melting, to watch them vanish over time,* I explain. You say, *I would stay for a long, long time, Amma, until everything was gone.*

Within weeks of our duplex move, Charlottesville erupted in protests and counterprotests over the removal of a confederate monument of Robert E. Lee. During a rally, a white supremacist drove his car through the crowd, intentionally injuring dozens of antiracist protesters and killing a thirty-two-year-old white woman. We lived a quick drive down I-95 from Charlottesville, in the heart of the capital of the Confederacy. The duplex was located three blocks away from Richmond's Monument Avenue, where a series of disturbing Confederate monuments lorded over the wide boulevard, celebrating a racist past that was in no sense behind us. At the time, Charlottesville seemed a turning point, a moment when there was no possible way those monuments could remain. But it would take three more years and the biggest mass mobilization of American bodies since 1968 for those monuments to be willfully transformed with brilliant public graffiti or pulled down by the brute force of protesters who had finally had enough. They are all, only now, finally "pending removal."

We laced up our sneakers and walked to the nearest monument, a bronze equestrian sculpture celebrating Stonewall Jackson. There is nothing interesting about this monument, nothing at all I could point to and say, *Look at that detail, the way the artist . . .* Truly, it was just another militarized white man looking regal on a horse. As we stood beneath the monument gazing upward, we talked about the historical role horses played in war. I told you that many were killed in battle, and you were instantly aghast, processing the injustice of animals being conscripted and sacrificed for the brutal undertakings of men. *Instead of taking down the monuments,* you propose, *they should chop off the men and leave the horses so we can remember them.* I'm compelled by this attunement, by the prospect of removing Man from the monument and letting the animal speak an alternative history that is already there, if we shift our public gaze. It is a promising displacement of Eurocentric history, a way of recognizing the animal—and those of us who have been animalized—by and through the consolidation of this nation.

Musing over your idea of an already-present countermonument, I found myself remembering the Jim Crow toilet in the Allen house, thinking of those monuments that are already here in our midst but that might be repositioned to envision the past and present differently. I wonder aloud over the prospect of taking this basement history, a history of debasement, and lifting up that dank old toilet as a testament to the country's abiding histories of dehumanization. The toilet, I suggest, could be a public reflection of the past and the present: an ignoble testament to the history of this place, a sign of the extraordinary shit some people have had to endure, and a reminder of everything and everyone we continue to lay to waste. In this strange fantasy, against the impulses and desires of the grand historical monument, I welcome the environmental and social forces that will over time act upon and interfere with this dank monument. That's the whole point. *That's cool, Amma,* you say, mulling over my vision, *but I still think the horses should stay.*

Years before your birth and long before I desired to be a mother, I surprised myself by issuing a spontaneous public declaration about the potential for parenting to be an act of radical pedagogy. A small group of graduate students had gathered after class at an uptown bar in Minneapolis. As we huddled around a table drinking whiskies to stave off the Midwestern cold, we collectively gushed over our young, female professor. We were being intellectually reared in a hyperpatriarchal environment where our professors were in aggressive competition with each other for scarce resources, where our exploitation—emotional and intellectual—was passively accepted, if not taken for granted. In starkest contrast, our junior professor's ethical sensibilities and personal boundaries were a welcome model of less coercive ways of teaching and of being human. She was a careful teacher, unassuming in personality yet spilling over with insights we yearned for. She was not particularly maternal, yet we collectively felt ourselves to be held in her care, by the rigor and generosity with which she approached each one of us.

We were eager to think critically about pedagogy, each of us in search of alternative models for what we might yet become. Nathan was more nuanced in his thinking about teaching than the rest of us, having already earned a graduate degree in education and taught high school English. He was besotted by Paulo Freire's *Pedagogy of the Oppressed*, where the Brazilian philosopher takes seriously the *form* of pedagogy, the way that dialogue itself unfolds. Colonial forms of learning treat pedagogy as information that is imparted from on high, Freire argued, whereas a more liberationist pedagogy could instead begin through collective dialogue about the actual struggles within a community, building slowly toward an account of how to make the world better for the whole. For Freire, the system of colonial education—the one we have inherited and currently learn through—is a dehumanizing system in which the learner is treated as a *thing*, an undynamic repository, an object of consumption. Freire wanted to imagine another kind of educational encounter, one that would humanize rather than dehumanize learners. Nathan, once a small-town skater punk and renegade animal rights activist, sipped his whiskey and declared that his desire was to push Freire's thinking beyond the frame of a humanizing education. *In the midst of human-induced ecological catastrophe, isn't it time we stop driving so hard toward alternative humanisms, and try instead to think about humanimal pedagogies? We need to displace the human at the center of our educations! We need to learn how to be better animals in intimate relationship with other animals! We need to learn how to learn as animals!* We laughed at his drunken appeal, but I knew he was right. He wanted to reframe learning not strictly as an ideology of human equality, but as an act of learning ourselves as earthly beings in intimate relation to other forms of earthly life. He wanted, really, to save us from ourselves.

As I nursed my drink and considered Nathan's intellectual treatise, I quietly remembered M. Jacqui Alexander's formulation of feminist pedagogy as a multidynamic act, one that might actually change the course of things rather than serially reproduce a politics of the same. In *Pedagogies of Crossing,* Alexander describes pedagogy as *something given, as in handed, revealed; as in breaking through, transgressing, disrupting, displacing, inverting inherited concepts and practices, those psychic, analytic, and organizational methodologies we deploy to know what we believe we know so as to make different conversations and solidarities possible.* Against the suffocating structures of our patriarchal educations, I found myself wondering over the capacities of pedagogy for making other forms of solidarity possible, ones among and beyond humans, ones I desired but had not yet discovered or lived.

The conversation veered into a tipsy collective decrial of human reproduction at the end of the world. All those present were committed to a politics of nonreproductivity, quick to declare that even beyond the heteronormative slant of reproduction, the world was so damaged and overpopulated that there was simply no justifiable ground for further breeding. Nathan admitted that he felt too damaged by his own upbringing to consider becoming a parent anyway, even while he admitted that he could imagine himself in the future offering sustained care to a child in need. I found myself wondering whether Alexander's account of pedagogy might also be the best summation of revolutionary parenting: as something given, something revealed, an act of breaking through, a transgression, a disruption. A way, in other words, of framing parenting not as a reproduction of the same, but as an abiding process of resistance and disruption. At the time, the parenting/ pedagogy relation was for me a conceptual question rather than a tactical pursuit. If I had stopped to think about it, I might have been embarrassed within radical queer circles to advocate for any form of parenting. Instead, I stumbled into a queer appeal: *Can't parenting be reconceived as life's most enduring act of radical pedagogy? Maybe it's too simple to refuse it outright . . . Why not engage it as an intimate, unrelenting experiment in unlearning the world we've inherited?* I could see Nathan from across the table becoming instantly enthralled by this formulation. A little fissure, an opening in his body as he realized that in all his monastic fervor, all his end-of-the-world solitude, he might yet come to spend his life learning with someone who was not-yet you. Learning himself and his politics anew.

I had a friendly acquaintance in graduate school with a South Asian woman of middle age who was married to a white man. When the couple discovered they couldn't have children, they decided to adopt a baby from an Indian orphanage. India has strict regulations around international adoption, making adoption of Indian children impossible unless you are of South Asian descent. The entire industry, both in and beyond India, is driven by a desire for infants, for children young enough that prospective parents can shape them in their social and psychic likeness. When my friend and her husband flew to India to choose a baby, they perused the orphanage carefully. After a while, the husband wandered off and started snapping photos. I don't know whether he was feeling some exotic artistic flare, or whether he wanted to capture the environment for posterity's sake, but whatever the case, an eight-year-old girl approached him, stuck her hand in front of his lens, and scolded him in Hindi about how white folks always took their pictures and never had the courtesy to return their images. With unequivocal authority, she declared this an act of theft. The white man was both taken aback and besotted. Returning to the hotel that evening with his wife, he asked whether she might consider breaking from their initial desire and adopting an older child. When the pair returned to the orphanage the next day, they discovered the girl also had a younger sister, aged six, and the couple adopted both girls and moved them to the American Midwest. I loved this story for how it narrated the unusual invention of a family, how a white man could be transformed by the rallying cry of an Indian orphan girl, sending history off its rails. How the story offered a lesson about the desires we inherit, and how these desires can, through unlikely contact, be remade and reimagined into other shapes and configurations.

One year into my new teaching job, and amid all the pressures of a ticking tenure clock, I had started thinking somewhat abstractly about family-making. My friend's story inspired me, and having volunteered at an orphanage in Jaipur one summer and fallen in love with all the kids, I wondered if this was a calling. One Saturday, I found myself driven by a strange Google frenzy, obsessively researching Indian adoption procedures. We were deep in the hole at the time, spending every penny of our monthly checks on bills and loan payments. When I learned that prospective parents needed fifteen thousand dollars in the bank to show basic financial security, I sobbed. Nathan was thoroughly confused, since we'd barely broached the topic of becoming parents. I admitted that I was likewise baffled by how something I didn't even know I wanted could strike such a feeling of loss.

The following morning, I was up early reading a French philosophical account of parasitism when I realized with striking certainty that you were crafting a world for yourself in my body. Despite my breasts being unusually sore, and my period a weeklong trickle that wouldn't fully emerge, it hadn't dawned on me that I might be pregnant. Five weeks before, Nathan and I had attended the wedding of my best childhood friend, who was herself three months pregnant at the time. I was honored with the task of giving a toast to the bride alongside one of Canada's most beloved indie rock icons, who would honor the groom. Needless to say, I was nervous, and before the wedding festivities began, I cajoled Nathan into a quick and efficient sexual encounter. It may seem ridiculous that it hadn't occurred to me that such an encounter might lead to pregnancy. After all, I had grown up with a host of televised public messages reminding teenagers that *it only takes one time.* But I was a woman in my midthirties, and everyone I knew at my age who was trying to become pregnant was doing so through a flurry of unpleasant bodily regimes. It took strange parasitic parables to reveal to me that I was, in fact, harboring my own parasite—that in the bizarrely articulated Victorian sense, I was *with child.*

I beelined to the pharmacy and returned home with a pregnancy test in hand, woke Nathan (who shared my initial disbelief that "the Toronto encounter" could become a legacy) with a cup of coffee, and went straight to the toilet to pee on a stick. At the sight of the unambiguous test result, our mouths dropped wide open. We headed into the living room, sat on the sofa, and burst into a fit of laughter. We sat for ages, just staring at each other. Then we laced up our sneakers and walked six blocks to the triangle-shaped toddler park, where we stood at the outside edge of a small brick wall, trying to invoke you through other tiny human animals at play.

That same week, my fifth week of pregnancy, we experienced our first hurricane immediately followed by our first earthquake. In between these climactic events, I began to bleed. I peered through my legs, watching gelatinous blood clots drop into the toilet as I dialed the hospital. The on-call doctor told me frankly that if I was having a miscarriage, there was really nothing that could be done this early in pregnancy.

You have to ride it out and hope for the best, he declared flatly before disconnecting. Still on the toilet, I called my mother in Canada. A former nurse and veteran of both pregnancy and miscarriage, she said in a sober voice from far away: *Oh, Jujube. You became attached so quickly.* I had indeed become instantly attached to the idea of you. I hadn't been planning you, nor was I sure I wanted to be a mother. But the moment I realized a little parasite was taking hold in my body, I also knew I wanted to spend my days helping a would-be you to thrive. In that space where the body and emotion become indistinguishable, I also knew that if you emerged as a living thing, we would each be forever making and unmaking the other.

Despite Nathan being an indispensable world-maker and my life's most abiding friend, his whiteness was never more fraught for me than it was during pregnancy. I felt an enduring discomfort over embarking on a procreative process that would lighten the human race in an era when we need a more capacious embrace of Brownness. Still, I had held a certain tenderness toward your father's whiteness ever since the day he revealed to me his profound fear of the sun. Sitting on a sun-drenched campus bench in the early days of our friendship, Nathan relayed that as a child, his skin would burn so badly that his body would blister and pus for days. He learned to shield himself from sunlight with an embodied terror. This confession—an indirect but no less poignant way of requesting we move into the shade—left me feeling an odd connection to him. As someone learning to critique whiteness with cutting precision, I felt surprising compassion for a fair little body terrorized by the splendor of sunshine. I grew to think of Nathan's whiteness as a kind of genetic weakness, even if it was one that afforded him incredible privilege as he passed through social spaces and crossed borders with what for me was an often-infuriating ease. For all our differences, we shared a fear impulse seared into the fabric of our skins, his born from the natural elements, and mine from cultures of racism.

Perhaps I am predisposed to having an ambivalent tenderness toward white bodies. As a child, what I wanted most of all was my mother's whiteness; I desired both to have her body close to mine and to become her body. I carried our racial difference across my childhood like dead weight, a second body I dragged along behind mine. From below, I watched the way my mother graced her way through social space while my father was met with hostility in the same surrounds. We are delivered into white desire, unrelentingly trained to feel its supremacy at every turn. I was in this sense born wanting to be a white girl, a desire that finally capsized when I stumbled my way into global feminisms and postcolonial studies, beginning to learn the histories that have shaped the world as we now know it. All this struck me as an awakening, a rallying cry, a summons, and a molecular relief.

In their edited collection *Feminist Genealogies, Colonial Legacies, Democratic Futures,* M. Jacqui Alexander and Chandra Talpade Mohanty write: *We were not born women of color but rather became women of color in the context of grappling with indigenous racisms within the United States and the insidious patterns of being differently positioned as black and brown women.* I felt for the first time in this collaborative feminist provocation the possibility of another world—a form of solidarity that not only bridged Black and Brown feminisms but positioned Indigenous erasures at the forefront of its politics. I was besotted by the idea of *becoming* a woman of color, in part because so much of my early life had been spent wishing away the lived experience of Brownness. There was a choice here, a process of emergence by which I could metamorphize within the very same skin. Global feminisms allowed me to sense and feel my Brownness anew, and in contact with those brilliant intellectual sisters and aunties, I too became a woman of color. I emerged as a body that lived into rather than against its difference. And so, while I had grown up with disdain for my racialized body, by the time I was growing you, I desired nothing more than to hold and be held by communities of color.

I return to this profound transformation often in your youth, watching you angle toward my body as I once desperately clambered toward my mother's. It is the same maternal love extending across generations—and it is also crucially different. You assert your unwavering love for the whole of me, not in difference but in likeness. You see yourself in and as my body—my belly your first home, my flesh the landscape of your intimacy. We have been shaped differently by and through race, you and I, and this produces in me an extraordinary feeling of joy.

From the very start of your life, your racial ambiguity has, like mine, hovered in the social sphere. The first time your father took you out into the world without me, a man approached you both curiously and asked, *Where is she from?*

In contrast to your father's blond hair and blue eyes, you were read by the stranger as a foreign body, a child brought from elsewhere. Unaccustomed to navigating race from the other side, Nathan was initially affronted by the question. He came home angry, a feeling that was at its core his first parental worry over your future sense of social belonging. *Did you tell him she came from the womb?* I asked. Then we chuckled, renaming my womb your *elsewhere of origin.*

Though you are lighter skinned than me, you identify with Brownness infinitely more than I could as a girl your age. Once, you were welcomed into the fold of whiteness when a friend on the playground insisted you could be white like her. You came home and admitted your bewilderment over this strange form of welcome. I described the stranglehold of race and racism, how lighter-skinned bodies hold more currency in the global economy, and I told you that your friend's insistence was in fact an attempt to situate herself in relation to other bodies. I explained that lighter-skinned Brown people are more easily digested by the white mainstream, that your friend's invitation was an illustration of the power of dominant bodies to tell you what and who you are, to situate your mixed body as they see fit. And I told you, there and then, that regardless of how your body is read by the world around you, you are and will always be Brown, not only because of the color of your skin but because Brownness is the unequivocal orientation of your maternal education.

We were smeared in whiteness. It was in us children, but not of us. It had disappeared in our mixed bodies but was everywhere in the cultural surround. Our mother belonged to that white world, and it was toward her coveted body that we turned. Born in Belfast to a scholarly Irishman and a Jewish girl from Berlin, my mother willfully darkened the human race by procreating with my father. She opposed racism through her body, taking pleasure in defying the order of things. The act of birthing four mixed children was in tow with much of the rest of her life's work: we were badges of honor, embodiments of her willingness to defy the dominant logics of white supremacy and anti-miscegenation that shaped our world. The act of mothering her hybrid children was—first by her choice, then by sheer necessity—unabashedly political. Reared through her fierce social critique, she taught us about physical and political bodies through a frank, educated lexicon. When we were wounded, she called our bruises *hematomas* and our cuts *lacerations*. When we learned to hate the color of our skin, she told us our Brownness made us more physically resilient, and that the white folks who assailed us were baking in the increasingly carcinogenic sun to look like us. When we found homeless people in the streets, she fed them at home and brought them to shelter. Seeing Indigenous poverty as part of our everyday contact with the world, she carefully explained the government policies and enduring legacies of colonization that made the suffering of First Nations people appear natural within the logics of Canadian settler colonialism.

As it turned out, your grandmother was herself a product of mixing, though of a more subtle kind, and one she did not discover until she was tipping into adulthood. Her own mother, a Berlin Jew during the rise of Hitler, had been sent away from Germany as a teenager. She escaped the gas chambers and was moved westward, where she would meet a significantly older Irish professor who married her and eventually moved her and their many children across the Atlantic Ocean to resettle in Montreal. Fearing for their safety in the midst of murderous anti-Semitism, and not prone to religious doctrine of any kind, my grand-parents told none of the children they were matrilineal Jews. It was not until my mother found herself drawn to Jewish culture and its young men that her godfather, a respected scholar of Hittite Antiquity, took her aside one day to explain there was a historical reason for her attrac-tion. I often wonder now over the role of the Holocaust in shaping her unrelenting drive to defy the order of her times. The discovery of being a Jew, and thus intimately connected to the unspeakable atrocities of the Holocaust, must have had a hand in producing her embrace of all life that was rendered disposable.

My parents lived out a highly politicized version of oppo-sites attract—my outlandishly feminist mother willfully cultivating a politics of the otherwise, and my father steer-ing sharply toward a pale, quiet assimilation. Because my father was born under the force of British colonial rule and surfaced into a world that was literally dominated by Englishness, his attraction to whiteness makes per-fect historical sense. English values, English aesthetics, English education, English government, English civility. As a Punjabi boy, he possessed none of these things, but was immediately trained to desire them. Whiteness was the ruling ideology of his world, something that from the colonized vantage point could be both desired and reviled with no discernable space in between. He loved whiteness, literally angling his body toward it by moving to Canada and refusing an arranged marriage in India to marry my mother. But he also hated its capture, the way it lured him in but forbade him from being absorbed. As one of the early South Asian immigrants to Canada, my father's turbaned self produced a constant slippage between exoticism and volatility, leaving him little room to breathe. Steeped in whiteness, he became a site of seething rage.

We never spoke to our father about race. We couldn't. Not only because his eruptive anger severed the possibility of that kind of intimacy between us but because we had learned our manners, and there was no polite way to explain that we struggled with the surface parts of ourselves that we had inherited from him. We may well have felt differently had we had access to our heritage, some form of Indian learning and belonging that could have tethered us to ourselves or bolstered us against our racist surround. Instead, we remained unanchored, fearful and ashamed of our father, and mired in isolated self-loathing. All we knew of our racialized origins was collapsed into our father's volatile body. All we knew of ourselves is that, as mixed bodies, we belonged nowhere and to nothing.

Anger, of course, always has an origin story. My father was six years old, precisely your age now, when India gained independence from Britain. The Partition of India in 1947 was a thoroughly reckless political process that led directly to the largest and most violent mass migration in modern history. (You will not learn this history in school, because America is stricken by a bounded narcissism, and because

Eurocentrism is designed to strangle its own subjugating histories.) The Brits were masters of a divide-and-conquer form of colonial rule, creating political turmoil between Hindus and Muslims who had lived in shared community for countless generations before the English took hold. Much like in America now, where the skillful cultivation of tension among "minorities" distracts us from political theft and corruption from on high, the English understood their power would be immensely strengthened if they created decoy enemies on the ground. It's a well-worn logic: if the oppressed fight among themselves, the oppressors gain infinite traction.

Before colonization, India had long been ruled by a series of princely states in which a diversity of religious communities lived with respect for each other's differences. Colonial occupation disassembled that system of governance and imposed an English political system, one that continues to govern India today more than sixty years after England finally relented. India was a colonial home to a Hindu majority and a Muslim minority, which means that as the country neared independence and prepared to inherit a foreign form of governance, it mattered who would take power. Keenly aware of their minority status and worried that a Hindu government would efface them, Muslims brimmed with separatist desires. The nation-state of Pakistan was born to house and protect Muslims from a religious majority composed of people who had once been their neighbors and kin. Pakistan, a name that literally means *place of purity*, was a roughshod colonial-era invention, a new Muslim world made by severing the right and left wings of the Indian subcontinent into two maimed and geographically dispersed political bodies.

The geographical borders that severed Pakistan from India had been drawn on maps behind closed political doors, offering civilians no way of knowing the actual locations of these arbitrary lines. The new borders were ideological cleavings rather than clearly demarcated spaces, forced political fractures that produced a critical ethical collapse around the question of belonging. There was news of rapid change, whispers of oncoming violence, a strange, seething feeling in the air. Suddenly, if you were Muslim, you no longer belonged to your Indian home. If you were Hindu or a member of the smaller religious community of Sikhs rooted in a place newly named Pakistan, you were now on Muslim territory. As independence neared on August 15, a communal frenzy set in, a mass fleeing, the clash of scared, angry, confused bodies in space, bodies abandoning their homes overnight because a colonial government had caused them to hate and fear each other, had wrenched a world until it snapped.

How quickly the world can turn on itself. How impossible to believe that where yesterday was love, today is a slashing of limbs, the mass rape of girls and women. Hundreds of thousands of people packed up overnight and left homes they had lived in for generations. Many were slaughtered in transit by an uncontrolled swell of misdirected emotion—a blind and terrified rush, a colonized force that realized in full its oppression through unmitigated murder, uninhibited rape and abduction, and unconstrained pillaging. A teeming, colonized body slaughtering itself into an independent future as its rulers gathered up their stolen wealth and headed home.

I knew nothing of Partition until my twenties, when I enrolled in an undergraduate course in postcolonial literature. I saw the word *Partition*, capital *P*, for the first time, and had no sense of its historical reference. It had never occurred to me until I studied the Partition of India that what came before, in other times and in other places, had such a heavy hand in forming and informing who and what I was. My own history was suddenly given a political frame, a way of reading violence not as a personal failing, but as a historical inheritance.

In the decades after 1947, those who survived Partition, including my father, remained mostly silent about this world-historic event. How does one make sense in language of neighborhoods and villages pillaged and burned? Of so many women drowning themselves in wells or setting themselves on fire to protect their bodies against the impending threat of oncoming sexual violence? Of women being abducted in unbelievable numbers, raped by men who had forced them to convert and become their wives after having slaughtered their husbands. As a boy, my father had watched the world around him turn on itself—friend against friend, neighbor against neighbor, stranger against stranger—torn apart by the whims of the British empire and the insidious politics of religion. No wonder he grew up rageful. No wonder this colonial inheritance left such indelible marks on us.

Shortly after my parents divorced, my father moved into a high-rise across the river that eerily overlooked our beige brick family home. It was an odd choice of residence, to gaze down on a life no longer his. Whether he understood this decision as a commitment to his own haunting or just the desire for a lovely river view, I'll never know. What struck me most about his new life was the sharp movement from a sprawling Victorian three-story to a densely populated elevator abode. As a twelve-year-old, I was baffled by the idea that he would willingly make home in a place that required access through a moving cage. I worried that he would be trapped in the lift, or that the building would catch fire and there would be no way out save the twenty-story leap into the teeming currents of the Assiniboine River. He seemed, in those early postdivorce years, to transform from a body characterized by volcanic anger to a soul treading in profound, unarticulated sadness.

Still, I feared him intensely, and for years after my parents divorced, any hint of hostility in his voice would cause me to flee, retracting for weeks or months before cautiously edging my way back into my unabating need for his love. Shortly after their divorce, I willed myself to confront the history of his rage. I had never intentionally provoked my father or called him to task; I had spent my life withering at his force. Sipping chai in his living room high in the sky, both of us tentative as ever in relation, I asked him point-blank what felt like a simple question: *Why did you hurt us?* His response was as revealing as it was withholding. He drew in his breath, then exhaled: *If I was not the father you desired, I am sorry. If I have done things to you that were not right, I am sorry.* There would be no moment of historical reckoning, no clear or conscious return to the wellspring of his anger. There was only this: two sentences that began with hedging *Ifs*, each followed by an apology. Still, it made space for something new to emerge between us, something that exceeded the grip of our volatile legacy.

I finished my chai and began to leave, but my father reached for my empty cup and refilled it. It was a clear invitation, but of what kind I could not decipher. Indian classical music was playing from his newly acquired stereo system, sounds that used to emerge from a cassette deck obscured behind the always-closed door of his den. As far as I knew, he never went to gurdwara and lacked intimacy with any form of South Asian community; nevertheless, I knew he was a spiritual man. *Are you religious, Papa?* I asked. As though he had been awaiting my question and rehearsed the answer, he said, *Religions are noble in concept, but when practiced collectively, they invariably breed hypocrisy.* I had never heard my father utter such a clear political statement, or articulate a thoughtful sense of the making and unmaking of ethics. I had heard so little from my father's mouth beyond the well-spring of his brute anger. I mulled over his words for weeks, then years. It was a message for my future, a way of saying, *You will never know the violence I have lived through, but herein lie the historical channels of our disgrace.*

In the purportedly multicultural Canada of the 1980s, I learned how to defend against racism through a rhetorical capacity to eviscerate my aggressors. The youngest child in a brood constituted by cutting words and quick fists, I was socialized to defend against aggression in all ways necessary. As kids, we protected each other fiercely from the racial hostilities of the outside world, hurling our words and bodies against anyone who dared to abuse us. But behind closed doors, we turned on each other just as swiftly. I was the weakest of the pack and terrified of physical violence, so as often as possible, I fought wars with words. When language would not suffice, I deployed my body and lost without fail. We fought hard because we knew no other way, because our youths were spent in the embodied anticipation of multidirectional violence.

Perhaps we were predestined to break, stemming from a genealogy of irreparable family fractures. We arose through and after Partition and the Holocaust, two world events whose legacies are as structural as they are intimate. My mother and father were both emotionally estranged from their kin, and following this path, became estranged from one another. If they had ever learned intimacy, they unlearned it through the reverberations of histories both personal and political. In this sense, breaking was our inheritance, something binding and preordained for our futures: to fall apart.

We began to splinter when I was ten, one by one abandoning the fiction that together we made a whole. My brother left home at sixteen, taking refuge in a tiny apartment occupied by four teenaged boys. My father followed soon thereafter, moving into a furnished apartment that would be his gateway into the high-rise life. Then my eldest sister, old enough to be on her own, was swiftly ushered out to make room for a steady stream of borders who began to occupy our old bedrooms so my mother could afford to keep the house.

At fifteen, I was the fourth family member to abandon the beige brick house. I left knowing that I would return a stranger. I lumbered through the years that followed in a state of unrelenting emotional pain. I suffered from piercing anxiety, though I did not learn to name or attend to the feeling until decades later. I scrawled my sadness into endless journals, vomited my way through time, overdosed on stolen pills. I was driven by unfulfilled longing: I wanted to know the origin of my father's violence. I wanted my mother to feel and reciprocate my gut-aching love for her, to look beyond our differences to the sensitive pulse that would always connect us. With my siblings, I wanted to show our strength not through acts of violence inflicted against each other, or through the compulsive need to cut each other down, but through the shared, humorous languages we had invented to sustain us against the world's unbearable force. I wanted everything I had no power to make manifest. I believed across my life (and still desire to believe, against the proof of history) that we could mend and shapeshift into relations that felt held and safe and loved. I accepted my parents' divorce without pause, and had no qualms about their necessary separation. But the fractures with my siblings were much harder to swallow. I desired desperately to resist breaking from them, believing that if only we loved each other better, if we cleaved ourselves open to and for each other, we might come through history otherwise. Instead, we did what we knew how to do: we forged bonds with the outside world and abandoned each other.

It may well be essential to our survival to track back through major and minor histories to select the legacies we carry forward. It may be our duty to collect from these embodied fragments, to study what has made us, then to decide will-fully what of it is useful in pursuit of a future we might yet survive. It is no easy act to know history so as not to repeat it. Following Saidiya Hartman, choosing our inheritances in the wake of extinction necessitates gleaning from the past, gathering up those muted, stifled, or stamped-out possibilities of living that might teach us to endure. This is not the sanctioned work of trained historians, but of intimate material bodies. It is not merely a way of refusing the distinctions between political and personal history, but of inventing other informed channels by which to live against and even into extinction.

It is no longer possible to look backward or forward without considering your body. I revisit the past through your frame, invoking in your shape the little human I once was, and all the other little humans in struggle whom we will never know. I look forward in time to a world in which I have become another body, a world in which my presence for you will be an absence. I look at you in the here and now to fabulate the world after this one. For now, I watch you calculate your surroundings, puzzle together a planet in ruin. And I wonder over what strange and beautiful practices you might invent to build collective lives and make them livable. How you might live through the breaks, and everything that comes after.

As I edged into my midtwenties, my mother discovered an international organization called No Kidding!, a social network of adults who had chosen not to reproduce for any combination of financial, ecological, political, and personal reasons. She found a way to weave No Kidding! into every conversation with her children. For a woman who herself had birthed four kids, her enthusiasm for an organization aimed to support nonreproduction seemed odd—even, from the viewpoint of her progeny, a bit insulting. Nevertheless, I understood that global climate change, which was by then undeniable to those not fully lulled into capitalist compliance, had produced in her an urgency to dramatically reduce the reproductive social order. She wanted her children (and everyone else's) to cultivate a desire for and commitment to nonreproductivity for the sake of life itself. Nevertheless, here you are on this devastated planet—the bright, beautiful, inventive fact of you.

In this same era, my mother mailed me an uncharacteristically sentimental greeting card. On the outside of the card was a sweet, cartoonish illustration of two squirrels frolicking around a wicker picnic basket, happily nibbling on strawberries. The Hallmark caption above the illustration read, *There's nobody I'd rather squirrel away with than you!* Inside the card, she had enclosed a newspaper article that she had clipped and carefully folded into quarters. It turned out to be a *Globe and Mail* article about the Great Pacific Garbage Patch, an island of trash that signaled, as well as anything could, the end of the world as we knew it. She had penned a note inside the card in her bold, beautiful cursive:

My Dear Daughter,

I couldn't resist this card! It made me think of you, especially when I needed some way of sending you the enclosed news article—which is truly interesting (+ SCARY). It is

*one more piece of empirical evidence that Marx had great
foresight when he proposed that the dynamics of advanced
capitalism would sow the seeds of its destruction over time.
In my lifetime I have observed many relatively rapid and
dramatic changes which suggest that the forces of capitalism
have, and will continue to, rupture the web of life to the
point of total ecological collapse.*

*And why aren't there millions of people protesting in the
streets???? That's the BIG question.*

*Love, Mama
xoxoxo*

If the card's message was an unusually saccharine choice,
the content perfectly captured my mother's particular
style of renegade parenting. For her, there was no maternal without the political, no way of being a mother that
didn't involve an urgent social and planetary pedagogy. To
be a mother meant to diagnose wounds and figure out how
to mend them. There was little difference whether those
wounds were to be found on individual bodies or within
the body politic. She oriented toward injury, finding broken bodies and restoring them, or holding them in her care
unto their deaths. This was as true for the bodies of her
children as it was for the bodies of downtrodden strangers.
As true for the urban forests as it was for the historical build-
ings, all under threat of corporate demolishment.

A psychiatrist in my adolescence once turned to me in
front of my mother, who was well known in Winnipeg
as an eco-renegade, and declared, *I bet you wish you were a
tree or an old building so you could have your mother's attention*

and care. I remained completely silent, but I answered to myself, *I only wish she could perceive my hurt as though it was at the surface of my skin*. My mother laughs at this memory now but was incensed at the time. Incensed by how the truth can sometimes pierce your body and make you bleed in defense.

My mother's drive to instill an urgency in her children toward social and ecological crisis—from the effects of factory farming to the brutalities of clear-cut forestry to the perils of oceanic microplastics—made her the perfect maternal embodiment of what Sara Ahmed calls a *feminist killjoy*. If I have consciously and unconsciously followed in her maternal footsteps by bursting the liberal sheen of social harmony and ecological sustainability in your youth, I do so in the spirit of survival. Yours and mine and everyone else's. Endlessly awed by my mother's form of maternity, I also understand what she often forgot, that sometimes a child needs to be held and loved well beyond the economies of injury.

In my youth, I worried obsessively over my mother's death. Not only was she significantly older than my friends' mothers but she reminded us often across our childhoods that she would *not live forever*—a double-edged mantra that served as a reckoning with her own mortality and a tactic for producing our guilty obedience. Despite this, for most of my life my mother's body seemed somehow immune to the everyday risks of living, and thus the unbearable worry over her death lived mostly in the realm of the conceptual. Over time, I've come to realize that what I find unbearable is less that my mother will one day die than that our relationship might shatter, both of us alive on this earth in a state of unendurable disrepair.

The sharpest memories of my youth are of sitting stealthily on the landing of the stairs in the beige brick house, eavesdropping on kitchen conversations between my mother and one or another of my siblings about my character flaws. My mother had a habit of sharing her discontents about each of us with the others, so that we were always toggling between the special position of listening to her dismay and being situated as the source of her disappointment. We moved swiftly in and out of her good graces, each of us basking in those fleeting affirmations, then suffering the evacuative loss of falling out of favor. It does not take a trained professional to see why most of my romantic relationships have left me in perpetual emotional insecurity, returning compulsively to a single looping formulation that cries out for my mother: *Are you there? Are you* still *there? How am I exceptional to you?* It's a losing game on all sides, a pathetic performance of endlessly sinking ships.

Of course, the marks I have left on my mother are likewise deep and enduring. She was cast out of her home as a teen, sent to live elsewhere because her mother found her daughter disobedient and uncouth. When I left her home in my teens, I inadvertently reopened that old historical wound, one that would never fully heal. When I left, history repeated itself through a perverse twist that situated her within a genealogy of mother-daughter breaks and left her flailing in the memories of the cast-out child she once was. She replayed her abandonment through my departure, living it out anew.

Although each of our relational breaks over time could by definition constitute a mutual choice, not a single one has felt this way. Both wildly sensitive creatures, we wound each other easily and have broken countless times across our shared history. Each break leaves us with an emotional gash, and each tentative return is a precarious stitch back into each other's bodies. I desire her and will always desire her. I look for her everywhere, discovering her now in myself as your mother, and also in the curious little renegade you are. The chronic breaks between us, the months and sometimes years of distance, have never altered the fascination I have with who she is, the urgency and fearlessness with which she has spent her life intervening in crisis and injustice. She is the central preoccupation of my life, the woman whose body made mine, whose ethical sensibilities are indelibly inscribed in me, and now in you.

When I was in seventh grade, a neighbor unexpectedly arrived at school to pick up my sister and me because our mother had been in an accident. As we drove home, I sat in the back seat of the neighbor's unfamiliar car, anxiously imagining her wounded body. It was totally unbelievable to me that my mother was a creature susceptible to harm. The accident turned out to be a rather strange one: She had just finished grocery shopping at the Superstore and had pushed a cart full of supplies to her car. Standing between the metal shopping cart and the back of our family car, she carefully loaded bag after bag into the trunk. Across the parking aisle, a senile man entered his car from the passenger's seat, put the machine in reverse, and rolled his car backward into my mother's grocery cart, effectively crushing her legs between the cart and the bumper of her car. Seeing the catastrophe unfold, another shopper jumped into the driver's seat of the moving vehicle and pulled the car forward, releasing my mother's crushed legs as she buckled to the ground.

The shopper who pulled the car forward disappeared into the crowd without receiving commendations. The car's owner, still sitting in the passenger seat, was bewildered by how he had come to be there in the first place. Probed by police about what he thought he had been doing, he repeated in apologetic bemusement, *I really don't know.*

When we arrived home from school, we ran upstairs to find our mother lying in bed with enormously swollen, gnarly legs. I had never seen my mother in bed during daylight before, and this struck me as somehow as unpalatable and confusing as the sight of her mangled limbs. Although she must have been on a dizzying dose of narcotics, she explained calmly and clinically that she had suffered a major compression injury, that the ligaments essential to the stability of the lower legs had been damaged, and that the unruly sight of her body was mostly the result of massive hematomas that would subside over time. The doctors, she told us directly, were not sure about the limitations the injury would cause to her future mobility. To walk, she strapped huge braces on her legs and pushed a walker down the hallway. Watching her, I noticed for the first time how an injured body can so easily mimic an elderly one. Soon enough, she would make an extraordinary recovery, teaching me my first lesson in making astonishing comebacks, so that when it came time for my own body to break, I understood that it was my inheritance to mend quickly and move on with things.

A year or so later, as my eldest sister and I walked our two beloved dogs in the neighborhood, an elderly woman in a cream-colored Cadillac drove past us and inadvertently ran over our aging fox terrier. Tuffy uttered a single extraordinary life-ending cry as she was crushed into the asphalt, and the woman drove on as though nothing had happened. She passed us with her white hands tight on the wheel and her chin pointed staunchly upward, her gray hair gathered in an old-fashioned bun at the back of her head, and her gaze fixed ahead.

Our younger and much larger dog, a terrier named after the Mughal emperor Shah Jahan, immediately began to howl in a tone and tenor that seemed altogether foreign to his body. My sister, a decade older than me, took control of the situation by bringing Shah to a neighbor's house and commanding me to run home to alert our mother. I ran so fast I felt my lungs burning under the pressure of my speed. When I swung open the screen door of our house, I screamed, *She's dead! She's dead! She's been run over!* And my mother (as a mother would) understood me to mean that it was my *sister* who had been killed. She moved so fast on those once-wounded legs, I forgot her body had been broken. As we approached the scene of the accident, my sister was standing alone at the side of the road beside Tuffy's body. I could hear my mother's voice surround me in a mix of intense relief and exhaled frustration: *I thought it was your sister!* It was hard for me to understand how the tragedy of the event could be diminished, how there could be a feeling of relief at the sight of our pulverized dog.

As we stood over Tuffy's body in a traumatic vigil, the Cadillac inched its way back toward us from the direction it had first come. The driver had taken a long loop around, plagued by a strange sense that she had *felt something* when she passed us. She had been out delivering Meals on Wheels to elderly people, she explained, and her mind was elsewhere. In our irreverent humor, we would later joke that it was she who should have been receiving the meals, but at the time what struck me was the sound of her quivering voice, the shakiness of her old white body as she tried to reconcile her intent to do service with the outcome of her mission. Her ethical orientation has always captured my interest, her willingness to return to a nebulous *something* she had felt, which seemed a frame for assuming responsibility even when one does not know with certainty that one has caused harm. Drawn to return by a *feeling,* she circled back with a willingness to meet the evidence of that something felt: a blood-soaked canine body on the road; Brown girls in tears with their stoic white mother, all hovering over the corpse; the sound of another animal howling with grief in the near distance. My mother assured the old woman that a quick and certain death was not the worst fate for an old dog and insisted her children would be fine as she helped the woman back into the Cadillac.

We set ourselves to the task of gathering ourselves, and gathering up Tuffy's body. We had never learned how to be collective, how to hold each other in grief. Instead, we watched my mother pick up a shovel and begin to scrape up the remains. Turning tragedy into a pedagogical lesson, she illustrated the parts of our beloved's body with each shovelful: *This is her liver. These are her intestines. This is her heart.* We carried Tuffy home in a blood-soaked trash bag, leaving a trail of blood splatters on the road behind us. We dug a hole in our backyard and buried her in our animal cemetery behind the shed. And then each of us set off alone to feel our way through losing her.

In the years after her divorce, my mother came upon a cartoon she clipped from the newspaper and affixed to our refrigerator. The image was of a bird lying on an analyst's sofa. The words in the bubble caption above the bird read, *My mother used to chew up worms, spit them into my mouth, and force me to eat them!* Mama loved this cartoon for how it played with the blame we place on our mothers for acts that are as natural as they are necessary to survival. Her gesture of affixing the cartoon to the fridge was an interesting one, not only because nothing had ever been affixed there before but because the fridge itself was a battlefield in our home. She kept strict watch over its contents, carefully monitoring what she put in and what was taken from it. She rationed our family's food, strictly governing what we ate and when. If we transgressed and snuck food from the fridge, we faced disgrace.

Displayed so prominently and exceptionally on the fridge, the cartoon felt like a defense against our future accusations of wrongful mothering, a way of normalizing what was, we came to realize, unusual maternal behavior. But it was also a way of revealing for us, long before we could understand, that the drives of mothers are laden with political and personal histories that make motherhood incredibly complex work. I am often judged for how I mother you, and against my own politics and desires, I judge others for their acts of mothering. This is totally useless social behavior, I realize, since we will all eventually be proven to have traumatized our kids anyway.

We had twenty-four hours to prepare for my last neurosurgery, a step up from the one five years prior when I was admitted to hospital immediately after my medical team received the results of my MRI. This time around, we had one full day from the time of the neurosurgical visit to being cut open, which was just enough time for Nathan and I to make childcare arrangements and to prepare as best we could for the months of recovery ahead. I had been warned that there was a risk my dramatic loss of mobility could be permanent, that I might not regain capacity in my leg and foot. The morning of the surgery, we dropped you at a school friend's house, and as I said goodbye, I feigned an ease that was nowhere present in my body. The moment you were out of my sight, panic set in about all the uncertainties of our future. Nathan, who invariably leans toward the intellectual (perhaps especially in times of personal suffering) tried to redirect my attention by turning to a recent text he had read by Donna Haraway, who was advocating for curbing human population growth. Haraway, he explained,

was envisioning a world system in which the population
explosion could be radically tapered if we moved away from
a logic of reproduction and toward one of kin-making. In
other words, Haraway argued for moving toward a model
of family-making without need for breeding.

An hour later, I was weeping on the floor of the pre-op
room. The ward had run out of available beds, and my pain
had become so excruciating I could no longer tolerate sitting or standing. Eventually I caved in, curling up on the
hospital floor. A kind but frenzied nurse found a bed for
me, quickly followed by a dose of painkillers. Soon after,
my neurosurgeon arrived for a quick visit before the operation. White, highly educated, and incredibly skilled, my
surgeon is a man characterized both by absolute confidence
and disarming humility. I like him a great deal and have
wondered over the years if it is accurate to call this form of
affection love. My feeling for him is strange and singular,
born of, in equal parts, his ability to command my trust,
my critical need for his skill, and his having been inside my
body in ways no one else ever has.

We marveled for a few minutes over how hard my insurance had fought to block my access to emergency medical
services. He outright denounced the health care system,
bemoaning the privatization of a medical industry that
had stripped away the ethical grounds of his profession
and declaring in no uncertain terms that doctors who had
moved into the insurance world, whose job it was to find
ways to deny medical access to folks in need to save corporate dollars, had sold their Hippocratic souls. Before he
left the room, I remembered that I had forgotten to inquire

after his family, and I asked how his two children were doing. He seemed touched that I remembered them and told me he had since had a third child, still an infant. I congratulated him, then asked if his hands were as steady as they had been five years before when he had last cut into my body. *Steadier,* he replied from the doorway without missing a beat, and it was clear he believed this to be true beyond a shadow of a doubt.

I saw him again as I edged back into consciousness from an anesthetic haze. He appeared with a young resident in tow, both floating by my bedside. He told me that things had gone very well, that the mass he had excavated from my body was even larger than the one he had removed with shock and awe years before. The resident, keen to punctuate the point, showed me a photo of the mass on his iPhone. I found the image striking—matter that appeared extra-terrestrial but that was in fact part of my interterrestrial body. I made the resident promise to send me the image but, perhaps unsurprisingly, never heard from him. Elated to be on the other side of emergency, I thanked my surgeon profusely, then found myself adding an inappropriate note of concern over his rate of human reproductivity. I told him that while I was certain he was creating a gaggle of little geniuses, I was also worried about the risk this posed for the health of the planet. He looked at me with what I can only describe as reserved tolerance, then turned and floated away toward his other pursuits.

I was instantly troubled by my impropriety as I swiftly descended into a state of overwhelming nausea. I waited impatiently in the post-op ward for his return, wanting to offer an apology, but a series of residents appeared in his stead. Once discharged from the hospital, I considered reaching for him by sending an apology note through the hospital's patient portal, but an electronic apology felt insufficient to transmit the sincerity of my appeal. Four weeks later, still kicking myself for my indiscretion, we came face-to-face at my postoperative visit. He was unusually behind schedule, and I waited for a solid hour in a claustrophobic examination room before a woman finally entered, discussed my concerns, and gave me the green light to begin physical therapy. By the time my surgeon entered, it was clear the visit was nearly over, so I wasted no time in telling him I remembered saying something inappropriate after surgery, that I regretted my indiscretion, and that I had been wanting to apologize ever since. Rather than assuring me that people say all kinds of crazy things when they emerge from anesthesia (a response I admit to having envisioned and anticipated), he looked at me squarely and indecipherably and said, simply, *Thank you.*

In the months of recovery that ensued, I thought compulsively about why I remained so troubled by my impropriety. I was undoubtedly rehashing my morning conversation with Nathan, inadvertently bringing Haraway's proposal for population control into the postoperative ward. Even more than Haraway, of course, I was summoning my mother's investments in nonreproductivity. Part of me wanted to issue anesthetic confusion as my alibi, but another truth is that I had wanted to say what I said in hopes of making him chuckle, to share with him a political concern about the state of the world. I believed in the ethics of what I had said, in the need to decrease our numbers and our consumptive habits, but the context was entirely wrong. Perhaps what was hardest for me was how my impropriety had revealed the odd truth that the intimacy I feel toward him is a wildly uneven one. To him, I am a body he cuts and mines, a vantage point from which my criticism could be understood only as insult. To me, he is a psychological and bodily anchor, a force that keeps me from paralysis. My wayward reach for him was a gesture toward a desired intimacy, a failed reach for his love.

My mother once read an article that predicted Canada would become majority mixed race by the year 2020. She saw incredible promise and took personal and political pride in this statistic, having been a forerunner in her contribution of four mixed bodies into the nation's multicultural mosaic. At the time, 2020 seemed like the space age—so futuristic, one could almost believe that a nation stolen from Indigenous peoples, colonized by Western European powers, and developed as an expressly racist state might become organically Brown over a few pro-multicultural decades. I found it hard to imagine that racial mixing, something that plagued my youth and bled insidiously into the whole of it, might become so ordinary as to constitute a majority. I found it even harder to believe that this future Brownness might produce a new, antiracist, decolonial Canada. I return to Canada now as an expatriate and indeed find infinitely more Brown and Black faces in the human landscape. Because my memory of this nation is steeped in whiteness, the surge of racial mixing and non-white immigration in the country feels to me both incredibly welcome and slightly disorienting. I ease my body back in, letting the reality that I am no longer an oddity wash over me.

I land in the Winnipeg International Airport, sail through customs with an officer who greets me with "Welcome to Canada! Bienvenue au Canada!" then easily accepts my Canadian passport as an unquestioned sign that I belong to this place. I travel by taxi downtown directly to the Health Sciences Centre, where my mother is recovering from a life-threatening hemorrhagic stroke. It is my third visit to the hospital in a month. She has been moved twice in that time, first from the ICU to an around-the-clock monitoring ward, then to the lonelier fifth floor, where staff visits are less frequent. Here, her life is structured around the timely intake of medications and the unbelievably cumbersome task of bodily evacuation. Each time she needs to urinate or defecate, she rings a bell and waits patiently for a nurse. Someone eventually appears with a giant machine in tow that hoists her limp body out of her bed and deposits her ungracefully onto a moveable toilet. Once she has evacuated and been wiped clean, the machine hoists her back into bed again. It is an amazing and disgraceful apparatus, both. *I would rather die than live without the ability to toilet myself,* my mother repeats over and over in those early weeks. *I understand, Mama,* I say, stroking her hand.

Decades before her stroke, when my mother converted the old beige brick house into a four-star bed-and-breakfast, our home was no longer our home. Coming back to the old house became an ever-confounding act of cohabitating with a sea of strangers who occupied our old bedrooms and moved easily through the space, uninhibited by the memories it assailed me with. My mother ran herself ragged there, up before dawn to bake muffins, to scrub, launder, and tidy until long after the rest of us had fallen to sleep at night. It was excruciating to watch, especially so as her body aged. When her knees became too worn and sore to bear her weight, we watched her crawl up the stairs, dragging the laundry basket behind her like a ball and chain. However outlandish, the spectacle was also deeply familiar as a lifelong technique of driving her body so as not to face what was inside and all around her. As the matriarch of the house, she catered to her guests in her own peculiar fashion, serving them gourmet breakfasts as she lectured them on the profound social and environmental impacts of factory farming, or the criminal sham of American politics, or the history of the Jewish diaspora in Europe.

My mother has no memory of the moments before her stroke. Our best guess is that, at eighty years old, on her way up the winding hardwood steps to the third floor to tend to the mess of her guests, one of her knees gave out. She fell backward down the stairs, taking the full impact of the fall on the back of her head, which split open instantly, surrounding her body in a sea of her own blood. Had my stepfather not arrived home moments before to hear her head colliding with wood, she would have bled to death in no time at all. She often articulates her wish for that fate, a wish I understand completely. As my siblings and I have watched her age, we've often discussed a collective wish for her to die in that house. She has a place-based feeling of belonging there that none of us share or have ever known in our own bodies. But we want the passage to be less gruesome, a quieter end in which her spirit simply slides out of her old body in sleep.

We spend our days together in the hospital dreaming of her return home. We know without a shadow of a doubt that the bed-and-breakfast days have come to a catapulting halt, but we avoid the topic because it is the most glaring articulation of the end of her autonomy. We edge carefully around the understanding that this suddenly imposed paralysis will force her to reinvent herself at the end of her life. Instead, we talk about the spring garden, the indoor plants awaiting her greenest thumbs. The focus of her recurring concern is that the garden will grow wild. I try to reassure her that there are far worse fates for a garden than time without human impositions. I brush her teeth, comb her thinning hair, then fill a basin with hot soapy water and bathe her body in full, carefully tending to every crease and fold. We watch the sun through the window warming the hospital rooftops.

It is spring, and the Winnipeg winter is beginning to melt away. She tells me she feels imprisoned by the room and asks me to take her on a stroll in her wheelchair through the hospital. We visit the café on the main floor and share an egg salad sandwich. We are heading toward an art installation in the atrium featuring the work of a retired Manitoba artist, an eco-acquaintance of my mother who has captured the prairie landscape through images of trees and grasses. The installation promises us a world beyond the one we are living in, an elsewhere to these weeks and months of hospital life. A Mennonite choral group has gathered in the atrium to sing, surrounded by the art exhibit as bodies circulate through the space in various states of motion. My mother and I are the only ones to linger, because the sound is beautiful, and because there is nothing else to do. I try but fail to stop myself from sobbing, and immediately appreciate that the singers, so fully committed to their harmonies, completely ignore my spectacle.

When the choir packs up to leave, we continue down the hall and stumble upon a commemorative plaque dedicated to Ann Thomas Callahan. Callahan, a Cree nurse who survived the residential school system, was the first Indigenous woman to become the head of the hospital's gynecology ward. Later, she would leave to work with an inner-city organization called Continuing Care for People in Need, dedicated to serving Winnipeg's Indigenous population. As we learn about the life of this incredible woman, my mother begins quietly to cry. I interpret her tears as admiration for Callahan's achievements, awe for her feminist activism and a life lived toward community care. But I wonder if she is also stricken by a feeling that, after all her own activism, all her life's endless political battles, she has not done enough in this world. As my mother's daughter, I already know this feeling—an overwhelming sense that I'm not living life to its fullest, caught up in useless distractions, failing to embrace the profound and transformative potentialities of the everyday. I want to tell us both that this is not our end, that our collective work has yet to be done. I want to say, *I'm not ready for your surrender,* or, *We can still change the world together.* It's a childish desire, that my paralytic mother should remain a stalwart revolutionary until she no longer draws breath. The truth is, I

will feel woefully insufficient without her, incapable already
of fulfilling her legacy.

We move on in silence, arriving at a sunlit hallway of glass
windows that ends forebodingly at a locked psychiatric ward.
To our left is a glass door, an Exit Only sign that warns us
if we leave, we cannot reenter. It's cold outside, hovering
around freezing, but the sunlight is a beacon summoning
us outdoors. Before we know it, we have sprung my mother
from the confines of the hospital and are on the lam. I wrap
her in my oversize scarf, take a photograph of her pleasure-
soaked face as she inhales the outside air for the first time in
weeks. I push her through the courtyard, down a driveway
to the street, and she realizes suddenly that we are across
from the immunology lab where my father first worked
when they moved to Winnipeg from Montreal in the six-
ties. Instantly awash in memory, her body is drawn back
through time in a place-based reckoning. She is recon-
structing the old architectures through stories of the racism that circulated within and around them. I try to capture
the details of the histories she offers, commit them to my
own memory, but as much as I try, I cannot travel with
her. While she is propelled across a half-century past, I am
lodged here in this timescape, tending to her frail old form,
unable to leave behind, even for a moment, the paralytic
body she has become.

We should go back inside, one of us says. I try to spin the
wheelchair toward the hospital so we can begin to find a
way back inside, but the wheels immediately sink into snow
and mud. As much as I maneuver, I can find no way out of
this bind, no willed strength or troubleshooting prowess,

and am suddenly struck by the weight of my irresponsibility, the sheer impetuousness of our escape. Just as my panic begins to take hold, my mother begins uncharacteristically to giggle at the predicament, and suddenly we've both erupted into fits of laughter. Seeing us stranded and in stitches, a passerby stops to help hoist us up the driveway and back onto the sidewalk. We circle the enormous complex and emerge on a busier street, where we find warmth and shelter through a hotel lobby that stands adjacent to the hospital.

Again in the main arteries of the hospital, we travel by elevator back up to the fifth floor. My mother will remain in the stale room for many more weeks before being transferred for months thereafter to a stroke rehabilitation facility. We share the elevator space with an Iranian neurologist, a Ghanaian nurse, and an intern from the Philippines. Along the way, we pick up another South Asian woman, followed by two young Indigenous women who are part of a collective that has been holding vigil at a beloved's bedside for weeks down the hall from my mother's room. When we reach the fifth floor, we exit the elevator and wheel past the overflowing vigil, past the nursing station, past the old white woman with dementia who sits outside her room and recurringly remembers an absent daughter. My mother says, loudly and proudly, *There are people here from every corner of the world! The hospital has become a multicultural universe! Who would have ever believed it when your father and I moved here fifty years ago!* She is immensely satisfied by this multicultural scene, made genuinely happy by human diversity even while her own life has become unbearable. Her satisfaction over this bourgeoning Brown world is a balm to me, her joy a pressure point that lifts the otherwise intolerable weight of her now paralytic life.

As I leave the hospital at night, I survey the swirl of Brown and Black bodies—Indigenous, emigrated, refugeed, mixed—that populate the space. I try to make eye contact with anyone who will have it, imagining how all of us might yoke together to change the course of history.

When I arrive at the bed-and-breakfast, I drop my bags upstairs in my childhood bedroom and climb into a bed hundreds of people have paid to sleep in over the years. It is haunting to be in the house without my mother, as though the building is a newly amputated body, and she its phantom limb. I close my eyes, thinking of this old place gathering dust, my mother's immaculate garden that will soon grow wild. In the face of her debility, I am struck by a profound awareness that none of this was ever ours to lose. I wonder over what it would mean to simply relinquish it all, to give it back to those whose ancestors once lived on this land, who lived along the river that rushes past the edge of the yard, for whom these ancient oaks and elms were once kin. Only they could ever love this place as my mother has across four decades. I fall asleep imagining my reach for these other bodies, turning my palms open in a gesture that says, *Here. I am sorry. Please take it back.* I awake at dawn with the same feeling, the same simple words.

I left Canada for the United States two years after the attacks on the World Trade Center, when a vehement hate for Muslims swept across America and immediately spilled across its northern border. I was in graduate school in Ontario at the time, and on September 12, 2001, I enlisted in a makeshift organizing effort to be an ally to Muslim students on campus. This entailed walking with Muslim students through campus, getting them to and from classes as swiftly as possible, positioning ourselves alongside and around their bodies in gestures of safety. Soon thereafter, a nearby gurdwara was bombed when a white nationalist mistook a Sikh place of worship for a Muslim one. The turbans, skin tones, and accents all made them indistinguishable to the homegrown terrorist, who would not have cared to discern between Brown communities anyway. In Winnipeg, the Sikh-dominated cab industry went into immediate crisis when white riders refused to be driven by turbaned men who *looked Muslim*. It became suddenly clear that, to a certain seething mainstream, I might appear more target than ally, that I might be doing more harm than good in imagining myself as protection for Muslim students, that it might, in the end, be me who needed to be escorted to classes.

If the moment revealed the shocking ignorance of North America, it also gave rise to a feeling of solidarity among those who had become perceived as terrorists. I had felt a growing affinity and longing for other Brown bodies, but this political moment swiftly revealed that by virtue of being prospective targets, we needed to form a greater whole. If 9/11 brought me into closer alliance with other Brown folks, it was also the historical point at which I began consciously to withdraw from a national sense of self. I found it hard to hold any sense of belonging, to feel deeply connected to a place that was brimming with racism, so unreconciled with its own histories: a nation that had not yet given itself over in service of those first peoples whose crippling subjugation was the ground zero of its emergence. I love Canada—the raw beauty of the North, the art and music that springs from it, the hardiness of lives lived there, the incredible differences among those lives. Yet its enduring histories remain an untreated bodily disease—like a cancer eating away at the social brain. Like acid, churning away in the guts.

You were born in a country anticipating the reelection of its first Black president, a young, mixed-race man who rose to power by garnering a great national hope for a more equitable nation. His public body hailed a future of racial unity. His presidential style was inextricable from his self-cultivation as husband, father, friend. He inflated the national spirit, made America feel like it could lift off from its cruel foundations. In the run-up to his first presidential election, I sat in a local café and listened to debates among coffee drinkers over how Black the president really was. As someone who had never been *enough* of anything, I found the debate not only specious but effacing; it was a game of authenticity that mixed bodies were made to lose. To my mind, the debates revealed little about the man, who had raised him, or whom he had married, and much more about a nation driven by polarizing identity politics that could find no resolution in mixedness.

Upon the election, America quickly conceded that he was, and would remain, *the first Black president* in the nation's history. The world watched him age across two presidential terms, watched his wife remain a portrait of grace and his girls grow into young women. As you grew, the political promise ignited by and through his body waned. He upheld too many of the country's brutal legacies, putting into stringent effect the detainment of foreign bodies and the bombing of civilians overseas, making his ethos of *hope* feel disturbingly selective. His historic presidency revealed something vital about race and its relations to power, about whose bodies could be exiled and whose lawfully murdered. Yet I wanted the fact of his Blackness, that he himself was comprised of histories of colonial force and global Black oppression, to produce a lasting ethical stance toward *all* bodies in struggle.

As I changed your diapers and tended you in your infancy, I dreamed of writing to the president an intimate appeal crafted through evocations of our daughters. I wanted to evoke those other children whose lives were being destroyed by America—its guns, bombs, and drones—while our children were made to flourish. I wanted his early political promise to extend to those bodies that had no legal standing in this country. And I wanted his frame of justice to reach into nations whose women and children had become the sacrificial sites of American empire. I wanted him to shape a world that his children, and mine, and everyone else's, could survive. I never penned the letter. I knew it would never reach him, and I understood that in pleading to change the course of history, I would appear from his vantage point outlandishly naive.

It is years later now. A real estate tycoon has come to presidential power, a reality television star, an unfiltered hatemonger, a maniacal liar. You are five years old. We have just traveled across the country by air, and are driving through the streets of Los Angeles. You are gleeful at the new surroundings, dazzled by the hot, dry air, the palm trees. Everything looks different to you. The car windows are rolled down and we are feeling easy, open, full of possibility. We pass a small cluster of makeshift tarps and tents on the side of the road, and you ask whether the streets here are also campgrounds. I explain that like so many other differences you are noticing, homelessness too looks different here. I am in the passenger seat, and you are buckled in behind me. I cannot see you. We are discussing homelessness as a political problem, which leads you to invent a new game you call "If I Was President." *If I was president,* you say with absolute conviction, *I would give everyone a place to live for free. I would make gardens all throughout the city that would grow food to feed us all. I would give everyone enough clothes to wear, and make sure their outfits suited their style. I'd make sure everyone had a friend.* I smile so wide from the front seat, a smile you cannot see. I love these moments when I am struck by our likeness and also recognize you as your own visionary thing. *You've just articulated the foundations of another world. I would vote for you in a heartbeat,* I tell you. You are gleeful at securing your first vote, but then remember I am not a citizen of this nation. *But wait! You* can't *vote!* you shout. *I'll campaign for you, then!* I retort. *Okay, good!* you say, satisfied. *I can do this, Amma, I really can. When can I start? How old do you have to be to become president?*

I arrived in the United States in 2003 as a student on an F1 visa. In my first semester of graduate school, I traveled home to Canada by bus to attend the wedding of a family friend. When the bus arrived at the US border crossing, all passengers were asked to disembark. As the guards searched my belongings, they discovered the assigned reading for my theory seminar, a copy of *The Communist Manifesto*. Of course I knew of the anticommunist frenzy of 1950s America, but I understood this fear of communism to be part of a rather embarrassing national past. Yet as the rest of the passengers reboarded the bus, I was detained and asked probing questions about my thoughts on the then-president and on the first and second occupations of Iraq. I was asked about whether I had family in the Middle East, and when I replied that my origins were South Asian, I was pressed to reveal my *affiliations* with the Middle East. I explained that there were none, that I had no family there, and that I had never been to that part of the world. Eventually I was permitted to reboard the bus, which by then was significantly delayed and filled with impatient white faces.

While I was unsettled by the experience at the time, I didn't register its future effects until subsequent border crossings, when I began to understand that the interaction had made me into a suspect to the state. My frequent travels to India (first to pursue my family history, then to study Hindi in graduate school) set off alarm bells to the guards of the nation. I was invariably held at customs and at times mistreated by customs officers. Beyond being increasingly drilled about my (entirely fictional) relation to the Middle East, I was asked why I could not simply learn Hindi online rather than travel to India for language study. After living in the United States for several years, I was told one day that I was going to be denied entry into the country because it was late spring, and the border guard did not personally believe I had the right to be in the country during the summer months, despite a valid F1 visa that stated otherwise. She held my passport in her hands and made a gesture as though to tear it in half, wielding a grossly inflated sense of power and a devilish smirk as she fraudulently informed me that I had *no right and no reason to be in this country.*

Hours later, after I was detained in a windowless room alone, a young mixed race man entered and explained that he was there to take my fingerprints and scan my retinas. He dabbed the tips of my fingers repeatedly in black ink, wrestling with the strange fact that I have unusually shallow fingerprints that are nearly impossible to capture. I have no idea how to account for this, but each time a border guard asks me why it is so, I feel conspicuous, as though I am concealing a criminal past in which I've filed off my fingerprints to better commit my crimes. This fellow did not ask why, but patiently tried and tried again, rolling each of my fingertips back and forth, back and forth. His patience made me shift my disposition, soften toward him by recognizing his status as a cog in the wheel. I apologized if I had seemed rude, and admitted I was desperately frustrated over my bad luck at the border. Still focused on my fingers, avoiding my eyes completely, he responded, *It's not bad luck . . . You're being racially profiled.* He told me he was half Korean, and he too had a history of being subjected to recurring mistreatment at the border. He said he would be *fired on the spot* for telling me I had been flagged in their system, that my information was now irrevocably in the hands of the Department of

Homeland Security. I can't remember how I responded, whether I thanked him for his risk.

You are four years old when a new president bulldozes his way into the White House, then promptly issues an unabashedly racist executive order titled "Protecting the Nation from Foreign Terrorist Entry into the United States," otherwise known as the Muslim Ban. Never mind the homegrown terrorists shooting up American schools every day, never mind the endless looping of mass murders enacted by white American men in places of worship and joy. Everything suddenly becomes a distraction from what is born and bred here. The nation turns to an imagined threat from outside to bolster and let loose a fomenting hatred within.

We've recently returned from the Women's March in DC, where we walked the apocalyptic streets of the capital on inauguration day, sirens blaring and helicopters hovering, police bearing down everywhere. The following morning, we awoke to join the feminist surge, the defiant vaginal throng. Now, we are gearing up for a rally at Virginia Commonwealth University to protest the Muslim Ban. Protests have quickly become a familiar landscape, part of the logic of our intimate lives. Before we leave, we talk with you about the Muslim Ban, explain its nefarious political purpose and its life-altering consequences.

What should we write on our sign? I ask, a marker already in hand. We are running late but don't want to arrive empty-handed.

No Walls! you reply, appropriately linking and collapsing the Mexican border deals with the Muslim Ban.

What else?

You think for a minute, conjuring the new president and his followers, then say, *No Meanies.*

I'm making an outline of block letters, sloppy, not my best work. *There's still room,* I say encouragingly. And you smile, looking right in my eyes. *How about "More Girls"?*

Yes, perfect! I reply. I quickly color in the block letters while you draw colorful squiggles and dots all over the sign.

We walk to the campus as a posse, you on Nathan's shoulders, me carrying our homemade protest sign. At the rally, we weave our way toward the stage to watch the slate of speakers up close. One by one, they claim their rights, call out the injustice of this moment, articulate the world they want, a world that has been catapulted backward. Of all the speakers, the students captivate me most. I'm taken by how articulate they are in their youth, how steadfastly determined to refuse state power. I feel angry and hopeful and become aware that I am compulsively reaching for your body. Somewhere off to our left, a journalist is inconspicuously capturing the event in photographs. At the end of the rally, he approaches me to ask for my name and yours, tells me he got a striking photo of us.

Later, we will see the photo online. I look fierce, my face tight and severe, my fingers curled around the sign like a claw. My right arm is extending toward you. A sliver of Nathan's face appears between my head and the sign, an eye looking off to the side, watching our surround. We've propped you up on a large speaker to my right so you have a view of the stage. You are towering above me, both of us looking in the same direction, absorbing the same thing. Your whole body is studying the scene, curious and enthralled. Your mouth and hands are slightly open, and your face is uninhibited. Your eyes reveal that you are preparing for something. It's as though you are learning the present and the future all at once, undeterred by the magnitude of each.

At my first social gathering in America, a group of six new graduate students sat around a table in Minneapolis, all of us strangers. Aside from me, all were white and American. Four men, two women. Because the graduate program was historically and culturally masculine, there was a clear feeling that the women at the table were there to represent the program's soft commitment to gender equality. In this sense, the gathering was, from the outset, a kind of public humiliation. By way of an icebreaker, a straight man awkwardly asked, *So, who here is queer?* I didn't open my mouth, both because I found the question off-putting and because at the time, I lacked any form of definitional ease. When nobody spoke up, someone else chimed in to extend the "diversity" conversation by turning to race: *I'm surprised they didn't let any people of color into the program this year.* I inhaled sharply, steadied myself. A man across the table recognized my discomfort, cleared his throat and shifted in his seat, then tried to amend the comment: *Sorry, Julietta,* he said, *it's just that in the United States, when we say "people of color," we specifically mean Black.* Leaving behind much of what I found egregious in the remarks, I asked pointedly how other Brown people in this nation were invoked and was met with awkward collective silence. It was crystal clear they had never considered, or been asked to consider, the Brown communities that were here before them, or those that came after.

A week later, on the dance floor at a house party, a white woman swung her way tipsily toward me with a drink in hand, introduced herself as a fellow grad student, spilled her drink on me, and declared in no uncertain terms I had been let into the program to work with her advisor, a reputable postcolonialist, for the sole reason that I was Brown. Aghast at the brute force of her assertion, and the drunken ease with which she could position me—a total stranger—as a mindless body whose only currency was its difference, I couldn't help but be confounded by what seemed a willfully blind racial economy. How easily I had swung from being folded into whiteness by virtue of not being Black to being rendered nothing more than Brown currency in a hostile intellectual environment.

A queer activist couple had been especially kind in helping me settle into my American life, and they extended an invitation for me to join their community support group. Within the group, they explained, they maintained a racial hierarchy of speech in which those who were the most marginalized spoke first. As white folks, this meant they would willingly concede to temporally withholding their own voices to center and uplift those of others. Wondering over the demographics of this group, I had a hard time imagining where my mixed self would fall in this reverse economy of speech. Would we all show up, scope each other out, and decide by our skin tone who had suffered most? I wondered aloud whether speaking first had any bearing on whether and how white folks could hear what was being said. My query seemed to grate the air around us, and the invitation was quietly dropped.

A few months before you were born, a seventeen-year-old boy named Trayvon Martin was shot dead by George Zimmerman, a self-appointed neighborhood watchman. Zimmerman was mixed-raced, born to a Peruvian mother and a white American father. As a mixed-race man, he had carried out the long historical work of whiteness by executing its drive for Black erasure. Bizarrely, Zimmerman effectively became a white man in the public imaginary because he had acted through whiteness, serving as a strange embodiment of white America's fiercely racist will.

Just before your birth, Zimmerman was charged with second-degree murder, and shortly after your first birthday, the nation swelled with protest when he was found not guilty. Martin's murder and its aftermath revealed something critical about the complexity of mixedness in this calculus, about how Zimmerman had lived and acted through whiteness: if an innocent Black boy's murder ends without criminal justice, it has failed to do the work it should have done to split open a public discourse about racial hybridity and the cross-racial antagonisms that unfold under the powerful lure of whiteness. Zimmerman appeared as a horrifying illustration of how whiteness magnetizes what is not Black in America, enacting racism against Brown bodies while also summoning them to fulfil its destructive will.

If one could hope in the face of unthinkable brutality, I hoped we might turn at that moment to crafting a history of Brown and Black solidarity against white state violence. I imagined a history that remains largely untold and unregistered within national consciousness. Not because it does not exist, but because the nation refuses to allow it in, to loosen its attachments to the racial binary. I felt the strongest desire then to write a real and imagined history for you, a chronicle of rescue and solidarity between Black and Brown bodies in this place called America. Or a love letter penned to every woman of color whose eyes have met mine in passing, whose smile in those fleeting moments has made the world feel more possible. A letter that might begin: *Dear You, I do not belong here, and I belong nowhere else.*

Four years after Trayvon Martin was killed, after George Zimmerman had become congealed as a white man in the public imaginary, I heard a knock at my office door. A sweet elderly colleague had stopped by to tell me she had been reading my tenure portfolio and wanted to drop by to applaud me for my writing style. I thanked her kindly. She lingered awkwardly for a moment, then departed. A minute later, she knocked again, saying she had just one question. She was confused, she said, by why I had addressed myself as a *female faculty of color* in describing my feminist work on campus. *I thought people of color meant Black people,* she said. When I explained that it was an umbrella term for non-white people and was not reserved exclusively for

Black folks, she seemed utterly confounded. *All these years,* she said, *I thought that Brown people were just considered white!* And then I watched a light bulb go off for her as she said, more to herself than to me, *Well, now it makes sense why my Indian cabdriver always calls me a white lady!*

In 2014, after eighteen-year-old Michael Brown was shot dead in Ferguson, Missouri, by a white police officer, we marched from Monroe Park to City Hall in downtown Richmond. The Black Lives Matter movement had just turned one, you had turned two, and you were both gaining critical momentum.

A month earlier, we had pulled into the downtown Kroger parking lot and stumbled into a rapidly escalating fight between two young Black men. I pushed you behind my body and reprimanded them as we passed, insisting they show respect for the women, children, and elderly folks in the lot who didn't want to be subjected to their aggression. Nathan immediately seized my arm, pulling me forward at a quick pace while scolding me for my brazen foolishness. When the three of us reached the automatic doors of the store, an older Black woman ushered us inside swiftly, where we moved through a handful of people who, fearing gun violence, had abandoned the parking lot to take shelter inside. In the moments after, and for days to come, you asked me repeatedly to explain what had happened in the parking lot. You had never heard me raise my voice to strangers and were baffled by the conditions under which I would do so. Each time you asked, I repeated the same story: Two young men had been fighting and had scared people. I had asked them to stop, which Nathan quickly reminded me had not been a wise thing to do. That folks inside the sliding doors were taking shelter for their safety.

We lived at the time near a sprawling public university in an almost alarmingly white neighborhood. A few weeks after the parking lot incident, we pulled up in front of our house, and, seeing a pubescent Black boy across the street, you announced that there was *a bad guy* near our house. I realized instantly the connection you were making between the men yelling in the parking lot and this boy, who had become "bad" simply by virtue of being Black. I unbuckled your car seat and lifted you onto the boulevard, then kneeled in front of you on the grass and told you that angry men came in all colors, shapes, and sizes. I explained that the anger of the men in the parking lot had no bearing at all on the goodness of this boy, that he belonged here as much as and historically more than we did. None of us is immune from the permeating force of racism, the reality that Black masculinity is cast as fundamentally negative in this nation. Still, I had a piercing feeling I had failed you, that in hollering at those men and narrating the scene back to you, I had misaligned you with whiteness by not detailing the racial, gendered, or class valences that made up the scene. I knew that in failing you, I had also failed the boy passing by our house, and failed, too, the young men in the parking lot.

The day we marched to City Hall, I told you we were marching against the systemic devaluing of Black bodies. We marched under the banner of justice, though I have always found this to be a complicated notion, one difficult, perhaps even impossible, to realize in a deeply healing way through appeals to the state. We were marching to oppose a state that flourished by making some bodies disposable, subjected to being killed, maimed, and imprisoned without need for reason or recompense. I wanted to explain to you that we ourselves had sprung up from histories in which our bodies have been rendered disposable by both fascist and colonial state powers, but I didn't want to strip away the crucial specificity of this moment, of Michael Brown himself, or of the Black and Latino communities whose deaths and incarcerations are the bread and butter of this nation.

In the immediate aftermath of the last presidential election, a senior feminist colleague visited my class. A white lesbian who lives her life through protest and acts of solidarity, she faced a room full of devastated Queer Literature students and offered them a brief history of protest in Richmond. She told them that even when protests appear to have no political effect, there is a crucial *feeling* in the act of gathering, of being together in a set of beliefs despite all other differences, that can be vital to bolstering individuals in times of crisis. I loved how she framed the need for coming together, which spoke to my always-tentative protest feeling, one that emerges because I am critical about how my public displays of activism dissipate in the everyday unfolding of my life. I feel uneasy about performing myself at public gatherings as more than I am in the mundane tenors of my life lived otherwise.

As we marched, we carried the weight of Michael Brown's death, and all the past and future deaths it summoned, feeling a sense of solidarity with strangers bound together by shared outrage. It wasn't a sufficient response by any means, but it was a kind of collective creation. When we reached the steps of City Hall, the police formed a half-moon perimeter around us. Their presence was not at all surprising, but as is inevitably the case when police violence brings protesters to the streets, the atmosphere was incredibly tense. I kept eyeing their gun holsters fearfully, when suddenly I became aware of another perimeter of bodies—a small row of gangly boys lined up together holding rifles against their chests. I felt my breath collapse and reached for Nathan, pointing my chin toward the armed boys. *Right to bear arms,* he shouted in my ear, trying to be heard amid the protest cries. *They are little boys!* I shouted back at him. *I know! But old enough to go to war,* he replied, illustrating the absurdity of it all. I glanced at the hard, uniform heft of the police bodies, then over to the pimply pubescent boys so keen to claim their rights, and felt a driving need to flee.

We left the protest swiftly, my body tight against yours as we made our way through the crowd toward the bus stop. As we boarded the downtown bus, the driver asked if we had been at the rally, and when we replied yes, he looked at us with intense, solemn eyes and said, *Thank you.* I wasn't sure if we were being thanked for caring about Black bodies in America, or if it was simply the shortest way of saying, *We believe in something together.* Whatever the intention, the bus driver's thanks lingered with me not so much because of its opacity, but because it had come on the heels of my decision to flee. The need was bodily, felt suddenly in the gut. Of course, it was not only my bodily need but my legal responsibility to protect you. In this sense, my urge to protect you rhymed with the fulfilment of my state-sanctioned duty as your legal guardian. There seemed to me something brutal about my not having a legal obligation to protect other people's children, that I could continue to protect you while Michael Brown's mother had lost this capacity, if she had ever had it in the first place. I felt outraged by the law, not only designed around the protection of whiteness but around a reproductive, nuclear family unit that entirely narrows the ethical frame. A punitive system that encourages us to stay small and bounded in our ethical horizons, obliged to protect only what we possess.

The bus driver's thanks opened me toward a series of ethical questions. Riding home, I bounced you on my knee and stared out the window, wondering how best to articulate them. *Whose bodies are ours to protect? Whose children are we free to discard? Who can flee to safety, and who gets left in the lines of fire? Whose worlds have been destroyed, and whose are soon to be? Does it make sense to distinguish between the child's body and the body of the earth?* I kept thinking that in another world—in a world after this one—you might be the child of every community under threat, and I might be a mother to every threatened child.

There's a Justin Phillip Reed poem titled "Paroxysm" I keep returning to wherein the poet reflects on our ecologically *wasteful epoch,* calling into question a voice that keeps warning against the production of ecological catastrophe but fails to account for the ongoing history of Black erasure. Reminding us that *an ocean of their bodies, beached— / were also of this world,* Reed brings the Atlantic slave trade to bear on the disappearance of bees and the dismal state of the world's oceans. One condition, after all, has given rise to the other; the slave trade and irreversible global climate change are two crucial pivot points in the history of capitalism. One where the global system exploded through the oceanic traffic of Black bodies, and the other where it began to undo itself by poisoning its wellspring and plundering the earth's nonrenewable resources.

Refusing to place environmental crisis over slavery's legacies, Reed writes that *the question of living becomes one of / committing to your own extinction,* then follows thereafter with an avowal that *you don't expect survival but / demand to survive nonetheless . . .* He orbits from the vantage point of queer Blackness, pointing to the ways particular bodies are forced to expire. As far afield as we may be, when I read the poem, I want little more than to join him in his commitment to a possibly inevitable extinction, to its oncoming rush, by resisting the mechanisms that are delivering us all to this perishing place.

If our survival has by now become impossible, I want to join all our expiring selves in fierce poetic refusal, until every last one of our bodies has been destroyed, then recycled, to emerge as other earthly things.

For many months after my first neurosurgery, I became obsessed with the prospect of my own death, of being absent to an infant and a best friend. I tried to orchestrate a life without me, discussing with Nathan how he might talk with you about girlhood, changing bodies, climate catastrophe, race, whiteness. He listened patiently to my proscriptions and advice for months on end as I directed him into this other world. I needed to anticipate how it would unfold, what shapes it would take. This all came to a halt one day when, embodying a real confidence in his unfurling relationship with you, Nathan declared bluntly that you would both survive without me. This clear response produced the strangest sensation throughout my spine. It was an utterly unbearable fact, and also all I needed to hear. It put the matter to rest. Such maternal fuckery, to find oneself absolutely indispensable and, ultimately, not needed at all.

In a similar vein, I remain afflicted by an unbearable habit of imagining your life in jeopardy. I conjure images of you being taken from me, then feel my way into the desperation of losing you. I often envision apocalyptic scenarios in which we are under extreme threat and I must quickly decide how to act: The world has fallen apart and we are forced to flee. Men are pounding at our door, demanding entrance. There are no resources left. We are going to be raped, tortured. We are going to be piled into trains and taken to extermination camps. We are on the verge of being separated forever. We are being burned alive. In the face of these apocalyptic scenarios, I consider how to end our lives humanely. I invoke quick and gentle ways to finish us off, to ensure we don't suffer or perish under brutal hands. I text my sister, an anesthesiologist, to inquire over the most painless and expedient way to end our lives. She reacts to the text with exclamation marks, then a day or two later, follows up by offering me a concise answer. It is all a game of summoning the worst so as to avoid it, which may not be so different from preparing for the inevitable. Do other mothers think and feel this way? Or is this dynamic violence in our blood, so deeply embedded in our history that it has taken root in our cellular selves, then emerged as an emotional condition?

As soon as you were born, the world around us began to anticipate another one: *God's gonna bless you with a boy next!* a stranger said to me in line at the grocery store. *I had a dream—more of a vision—that you are going to have another child, a son!* a kindhearted colleague declared at work one morning. *It's the greatest joy of your life,* someone I do not remember said to me, *and the beauty is that you get to do it again and again!* Lest I forget the social chorus that has always sung, *You don't want her to be left all alone in the world when you're dead and gone, do you?*

A friend once confessed she felt pressure to have a second child because she feared her life would fall apart if her first-born were to die. She needed a backup, something to hold her together in the case of his untimely death. I found my friend's formulation intriguing, mostly because it worked against the common logics and social pressures for pro-ducing multiple children. Stripping away the social fictions that inform a perceived need for a four-part nuclear family, my friend understood that it was her own worry, her own psychological need, that gave rise to a desire for another child—a second child positioned to become an only child if its mother's worst fears were realized.

I have not offered you a sibling, and in turn, you have not asked for one. I've learned that biological siblings are by no means a guarantee of the kinds of support and love you will need, that the bonds you craft yourself will be the fires that ignite you. For now, you consider Mars and Sprit, the jet-black rescue kittens who mostly live downstairs with your father, and our nearly toothless stray dog, Ellery, your siblings. I see this trans-species siblinghood not as a childish displacement of your desire for "real" siblings but as a sign of your keen capacity to find and make networks of belonging that do not hinge on biological affiliation or the anthropocentric conventions of the nuclear family. I take promise in your ability to craft kinships, to be a support for and supported by the worlds you help shape, however unconventional they may be.

Last weekend, as we walked our dog at dusk, you revealed you had a secret to share with me about a school friend's father. As we passed other pedestrians, you made a show of *waiting for the coast to clear* so that not a single other soul would hear you. *It isn't safe for anyone else to know,* you said. You made me solemnly swear to keep the secret, then whispered into the night air, *K's father is in prison.* You elongated the word *prison,* voicing it like a bereavement song. You looked over your shoulder, then all around us, before proceeding. *He grabbed a Taser from her mother and tased someone in their house while K was in her bedroom.* I felt uneasy hearing the word *Taser* emerge from your mouth, a word I was certain you didn't understand. *K's mother must be a police officer,* you added, a detail I found odd and wouldn't understand until weeks later.

You insisted we share this secret with no one other than Nathan. It was *especially important,* you said, to hide this information from people who work for big companies. Big companies have spies, and spies could get K's father into trouble. I posited that K's father was already in deep trouble by virtue of having been incarcerated, and told you that an extraordinary number of people, especially Black and Latino men, are incarcerated in this country, and the number of incarcerated women of color is steeply on the rise. I told you the criminal justice system has nothing to do with justice, that in fact, it is a vast and unbelievably profitable network. And then I turned our attention to K, who I said must be feeling scared and confused. *She's so sad,* you say, *but her supernice grandma has come to live with them while her father is in prison. Sometimes her grandma comes to school at lunchtime and buys K an ice cream from the cafeteria.* In this sense, you suggest that K is also quite lucky.

Later, I google *Tasing* and find a nearly three-minute-long video montage of a host of white policemen engaging in a perverse pleasure-torture game. Two men stand on either side of a third man, bracing his arms. Off camera, a voice shouts, *Taser! Taser! Taser!* like an incantation, before the man in the middle endures several seconds of tasing and an unseen crowd hollers and cheers. Most of the men being tased stay frozen with intense scowling faces, then let out a big breath of relief as their bodies pulse in the aftermath. Toward the very end of the video, a slim policewoman appears. Like the tased men, she is positioned between two male officers. She looks as stoic and braced as the men who have come before her, but as she is tased, she throws her head back so the viewer cannot see her face. She endures the tasing, her face clenched to the sky, until it is over and she collapses forward, looking like she is going to vomit or cry. The officer to her left pats her shoulder gingerly and says, *Good job!*

I try to understand the nature of this game, the lessons embedded in this ritual. Are the police officers learning what it feels like to be tased so they are prepared to endure it on the job? Are they learning empathetically how it feels to do what they will do to other bodies? Or is this simply a team-building exercise to show each other that they are strong, that they can take it, that there is no weakness in this fraternity? Perhaps all three. Whatever the case, the video has more than 2.5 million views, which I believe by definition means it has *gone viral.*

If tasing has been fixed in the popular imagination through viral visions of police brutality, it has now entered yours as a word synonymous with violence. *He grabbed a Taser from her mother and tased someone in their house while K was in her bedroom.* I was left wondering what this narrative scene looked like in your mind, how a child imagines a weapon she has never seen. But when I approach Nathan to discuss the oddity of you speaking of tasing without a conceptual framework for it, I am stunned to learn from him that you have, in fact, recently encountered a Taser through a Girl Scout troop encounter with the police. The troop had been scheduled to meet a police horse and a police dog, to learn how animals are employed in the service of state discipline, but when the animals failed to appear due to a scheduling glitch, a policewoman improvised by showing the fleet of little girls her various weapons. (Hence, I realized retrospectively, your speculation that K's mother was an officer of the law.) I have been hesitant about your involvement with the Girl Scouts since kindergarten, when you asked to be enrolled with your friends. So steadfastly white in its citizenry, disposition, and spirit of state and corporate compliance, I felt nearly as tentative about this as I did about you starting your formal education. Perhaps unfairly so, the Girl Scouts has become emblematic for me of your acculturation into civil whiteness.

I love, of course, the idea of an abiding gathering of girls. What I desire, though, is a network by which politically motivated women and girls think together carefully and critically about the structures and ideologies that are actively shaping our lives. I want an East Coast version of the Radical Monarchs, an Oakland-based organization established by Brown and Black mothers to ensure their daughters are reared within the legacies and histories of our struggles against state power, taught not through white civility and liberal citizenship but through modes of critical resistance. (It's worth noting here that the Radical Monarchs were formerly known as the Radical Brownies, perhaps the best name ever bestowed upon a girl posse, before the Girl Scouts politely requested they change their name so as not to be confused with their own longstanding Brownie troops.) In your earliest youth, I was immediately besotted to learn of this alter-organization, which taught not only histories of political struggle but topics such as the enduring effects of state racism, violence against trans and gender-nonconforming people, and the aesthetics of Black and Brown beauty. I imagined a slightly older you on experimental field trips inspired by social justice and collective empowerment. Not immersed in an ethos of selling cookies and reproducing mainstream capitalist values, but activated by and through a consciousness of our own empowerment, the transformative possibilities of our collective selves. Most of us who were socialized within the consumptive force of whiteness (which is, really, all of us) did not encounter this counterpolitics until we neared adulthood. And we know, from this vantage point, that there's no time left for late political awakenings, no room anymore for the protection of an innocence that has always been exclusively reserved for white youth anyway.

Shortly after you revealed your secret Taser story, I drove you to the suburbs to participate in a Girl Scouts self-defense class. It was my first postsurgery drive, and I was feeling uneasy about the journey, in part over my capacity to get us there safely, and in part over how the notion of self-defense would be rendered for you. When we arrived, I was surprised to find that in a room filled with girls, the self-defense teacher was a hulking blond man, a proud eighth-degree black belt who looked like a retired US marine. He began the lesson by asking the troops to define a bully. After a series of hilarious responses from the girl crowd, he defined a bully as someone who repeatedly harasses you, who uses his force to make you feel small. He proceeded to insist it was never okay to keep secrets from your parents, and that if you were being bullied, it was imperative that you tell them. He built his lesson around the idea of an "us": *Together, we are stronger than any bully,* he declared over and over again. I could not help but to think of the US president, who fit this bully description perfectly, and wondered over what forms of collective strength "we" would need to overcome him. I wondered, too, over the self-defense teacher, over what circumstances he and I might emerge as a collective "we."

When it was time for the practice of self-defense, the teacher brought forward a woman as his victim. She herself appeared to be highly skilled at martial arts, and while she made big, effective gestures in response to his attacks, she never once uttered a single sound. She was so silent, in fact, that I began to wonder if she was mute. Either this, or a pedagogical decision had been made to render the victim entirely speechless for the sake of the lesson itself. Whatever the case may have been, the teacher towered over his silent victim and showed the Girl Scouts how they could break free from any grasp. He modeled a self-defense that invariably ended not by kneeing the assailant in the testicles, as I had learned long ago, but by poking the assailant in the eyes, then fleeing to find help.

Never, ever, trust a man, the hulking martial arts teacher told you. *If you run for help, run to a woman. Run into a public place and find a woman. But never ever run to a man on the street for help.* He then proceeded to confess that he had been waiting his whole life for an opportunity to serve girls and women in danger, to flatten the assailants who desire to harm us. I pondered what it meant to you, to be taught by a man how to defend yourself while all at once being told never to trust someone who fits his profile. The mixed messages embedded in the lesson not only left us understanding our place as prospective gendered victims but also left me wondering where the martial arts teacher situated himself in this economy of violence. A vision of full masculinity, he warned us against himself, all the while positioning himself as our hero. As the lesson progressed, you were asked to imagine a scenario in which you and I were both under attack. The teacher told you that you must abandon me, that you must run for help, that if you stay with me, I will not leave you and will therefore be further harmed. *If you leave your mother,* he said, *she will have the will to escape.* The lesson is forceful and clear: you must break from me to save yourself, abandoning me to save us both.

The incision on my lower back ached and pulsed as we buckled ourselves into the car and left the martial arts studio behind. As I pulled onto the highway, I caught a glimpse of you in the rearview mirror watching the sunset through your window. The evening light cut across your face, making you appear older, more severe.

I grew up under the ever-present threat of patriarchal violence, and the vast majority of my childhood memories are constructed around scenes in which I witnessed or was subjected to it. I did not need to be taught this form of violence, because I absorbed it as the environmental surround of my early home life. You, in contrast, are learning gender violence through various forms of pedagogy, being trained to anticipate what is bound to come your way not by experiencing it within the intimate confines of your life, but by preparing for it in the world beyond your family home. What you are learning is that one day your body will be subjected to violence, and that you must know how to defend against these impending assaults. You are learning that you will need to harm another body to save your own. The brutal fact is that there is a near certainty you will indeed be harmed—more or less egregiously—by the bodies of boys and men who have learned of your body as their possessive domain. I cannot name the feeling this fact produces in me, cannot parse whether it is an explosive feeling or an imploding one, the wild mounting of my physical rage, or my entire body in collapse.

We have been reading poems in bed together at night, reciting stanzas aloud in turns until each poem is finished. You keep calling the stanzas *paragraphs,* and when Nathan walks past and hears this slip, he tells you the word *stanza* is Italian for *rooms. When you read a poem,* he says, *you are moving through little rooms.* His tone reveals the beauty he finds in this linguistic formulation.

Last night, we read a Naomi Shihab Nye poem called "What People Do." You begin the poem, claiming the first stanza as your own:

> *November   November   November   the days crowd together*
> *like families of leaves   in a dry field*
> *I pick up a round stone   take it to my father*
> *who lies in bed waiting for his heart to mend*
> *and he turns it over and over in his hands*

I witness your interest in the repetition of *November,* in the familiar gesture of picking up stones, a gentle awe at the idea that someone in the world might be waiting for their heart to mend. Now it's my turn:

My father is writing me the story of his village
He tells what people did   in another country
before I was born   how his best friend was buried alive
and the boy survived two days in the ground
how my father was lowered into a well on ropes   to discover
clay jars a thousand years old   how each jar held seeds
carob and melon   and the villagers chose secrecy
knowing the British would come with trucks and dig up their town

Your eyes are wide and your mouth agape when you hear of a boy buried alive, his unbelievable survival, and your thrill is unabating as I read of the poet's father lowered into an old well to discover ancient pasts, the need to *choose secrecy* to protect against ravaging colonial desires.

When we finish the poem, you ask if we can read it again and switch the order, so that this time I begin *November November   November,* and you get to read the parts that most thrill you. As we reread, I wonder how the poet's life has been shaped by her father's stories, how his Palestinian village and its minor histories touch her life in its everyday unfolding. Which is also a way of wondering how my own life has been shaped by the stories I know and will never know of my own father's past, his world and its secrets. Perhaps all these epistolary pages penned to you are simply a way of offering you what I wish I had for myself—words to travel across a genealogy of difference. Rooms that came before and will shelter you. A kind of offering that is, by necessity, insufficient. A map to move you toward other possible worlds.

This time around, it's your turn to read the final stanza:

> *I would tell my father*
> > *I cannot move one block without you*
> > *I will never recover from your love*
> *Yet I stand by his bed saying things I have said before*
> *and he answers   and we go on this way*
> *smoothing the silences*
> *nothing can heal*

Even though you've already heard these words, reading them aloud yourself makes you consider them differently, allows them to take on new meanings. *Why doesn't she just say what she wants to say to her father?* you ask. *Because we get caught up in our habits, and can't always bring ourselves to reach differently for those we love.* I'm not sure you understand my words, but at least for now, you nod, satisfied.

Dadiji, my father's mother, a tiny old woman wrapped in a sari, a widow whose husband had died an untimely death, visited Canada only once, when I was a girl your age. She spoke no English but nevertheless made her love for me abundantly clear. I had badly sprained my ankle just before her arrival, and during her stay my foot and ankle remained expertly wrapped in a Tensor bandage. This was often the case in my youth, riding out some injury or another, which made me feel special rather than inept. Intuitively, Dadiji knew to offer me extra love.

One night, after soaking in a hot bath and thinking excitedly about her welcome foreign presence in our home, I forgot completely about my injury and stepped out of the bath directly onto my injured ankle. I howled in pain and crumpled onto the bath mat. My father burst into the bathroom fuming, enraged by my absentminded stupidity and the shameful scene I had created during his mother's visit. I fell immediately silent, absorbing the verbal blows, then noticed Dadiji in the doorway shaking her head quietly, dismayed by the spectacle of her son's rage. It meant something to me, that she could cut through the scene to relocate the wrongful gesture, that she saw I was not the offending actor in the scene.

The next morning, pointing to a picture of an elephant on the printed curtains in my brother's bedroom, she repeated the word *hathi* over and over until I understood, memorized the word, and never forgot it. Nearly thirty years later, *hathi* would become the first word you learned for elephant, a tribute to a quiet matriarch I never saw again.

When my father called two decades later to tell me that Dadiji had died, his voice sounded clinical. *My ties to my family are over,* he said. *I owe nothing to them now. Nothing to my siblings, and nothing to my children. My duty in this world is done.* I wept into the phone, overwhelmed by the loss of a woman I had met only once, and by the unbearable fact I had missed the chance to know her as an adult. I was stunned by my father's economic calculation, that with his mother's death came a kind of freedom, a felt sense he no longer *owed* us anything. Who were we, after all, this gathering of strangers? I did not know his family—his siblings were mostly nameless, faceless people, with nameless, faceless children—yet I felt suddenly connected to them by virtue of us all being collectively released from something he called his duty. *Aren't you saddened by her death?* I asked with an unconcealable ache in my voice. *We all die, kid,* he said soberly before he disconnected. It would be years before I began to understand what it had meant for him to be the eldest son of a large Indian family, what it meant that he went abroad and stayed there, felt himself to be little other than a foreign bankroll to his family. How alien he had felt in a white world, how trapped he was by the strangleholds of a thing called *family duty.* He never stopped supporting me when I needed help of any kind; he never cut our tie. But there was something important for him at that moment in the performative gesture of saying so.

I went in search of my father in my early twenties, setting off for India to discover his past, a place both entirely foreign and also somehow mine. My aim was to locate the source of his anger, to make better sense of him and, by extension, our fractured family. I saved up for a year while working a low-wage job at a furniture store, then quit, hawked my CD collection at the local record store, bought a backpack and a pair of ill-fitting hiking boots, and flew across the world. My sense of India at the time was entirely Orientalist, derived not from detailed family histories but from popular representations of India's exoticism, overpopulation, and poverty. In my pocket, I held a piece of folded paper with the contact information of aunts and cousins who were strangers to me, whose lives I did not yet know.

I awoke on the airplane to the godlike voice of our pilot instructing us to look out into the darkness. Below us, he said, was the border between India and Pakistan. I wiped the sleep from my eyes and peered out the window in awe, the border lit up like a flaming orange snake. I knew my father had been born in a village that was now part of Pakistan, and had as a boy migrated with his family to the other side of that border around the time of Partition. I knew this beautiful orange snake, almost artistic in its expansiveness, was also a wound—a political gash that had made a staggering number of bodies bleed, burn, and cave in to the future. I had felt its effects across my life long before I knew its history. I realized I was weeping only when the old Indian woman beside me patted my back gently and handed me her oily handkerchief.

If I have always felt myself to be an alien body, this feeling was never more palpable than when I arrived for the first time in my father's homeland. My body seemed to scream its unbelonging at every turn. Even in a salwar kameez with a scarf covering my short hair, my foreignness shone through simply by the way I moved through space. My Punjabi relatives embraced me with the widest and most open arms, welcoming me as their daughter and sister. They offered me an unfamiliar form of love—a love bestowed through the simple fact that I was my father's daughter— and I didn't know how to trust it. My aunties and cousins made it their duty never to leave my side, treating me like the cultural infant I was. I didn't know how to use the toilet, how to take a bath, how to eat and drink safely, how to hail a rickshaw, or how to buy basic necessities at the market. I didn't know how to make my body inconspicuous and was a walking target for unwanted attention.

I stayed with my newly found family for weeks in a kind of cocoon that both buffered me from culture shock and left me feeling stifled by the degree of their care. I shared a bed with my father's eldest sister, my bhuaji, whose face was a warmer and fleshier version of his. We spent endless hours lying on the bed together, talking about him. She told me her brother's unexplained disavowal of the family was the greatest heartbreak of her life. As a boy, she said, he was the most jovial of all the children, a prankster who kept everything lively. The two of them, as eldest siblings, had been especially close. When he left for Canada in his early twenties (around the same age I was at the time), he changed in ways that left her mystified. When she spoke of him, she wept, repeating in her thick Punjabi accent a one-word question: *Why?* We talked of him as though he was dead, but calculating the time difference, I knew he was sitting in his living room, his long legs crossed, listening to Sikh devotional songs while sipping his morning chai.

It turned out my Indian family needed from me the same thing I had traveled across the world to glean from them: a way to explain the enigmatic man who held critical distance from us all. Realizing there were no answers to be found in our discourse, I asked if we could travel five hours by car to Amritsar to visit the family's former home. I knew very little of this place, but remembered a single story my father used to tell about planting a mango tree in the yard as a boy and eating its fruit across his youth. When we ate mangos in my childhood, he would invariably tell me to go outside and plant the pits in the Canadian soil, as though I might magically reproduce his past. In Amritsar, I meandered across the terrace of his now decaying home, trying to conjure my father as a carefree boy. His sisters described how they all used to sleep on the veranda on hot nights, how my father the prankster used to keep them up at night with his shenanigans. I searched the yard and found a single mango tree that bore no fruit. I kneeled before it like an unmarked grave and bowed my head to the earth. The gesture was somewhere between an act of mourning for the boy I never knew, and one of conjuring him from the past to guide me through this time and place.

We left the house and traveled a short distance to the memorial site of the 1919 Jallianwala Bagh massacre. A commemorative plaque explained that under the command of Reginald Dyer, British Indian Army troops had opened fire there on peaceful protesters. I wandered around the public memorial, trying to understand my place in this gruesome history. I peered into a deep, wide well. Beside it, another plaque marked that this was the site where dozens of peaceful civilians seeking political change had jumped in and drowned in a collective attempt to avoid the murderous gunfire of the colonial regime. I felt sick and wanted to go home, but the whole notion of "home" had become critically opaque.

After Amritsar, I left my family to become a tourist, traveling north toward the Himalayan mountains. My bhuaji had awoken early to make me a stack of chapatis, which she wrapped in tinfoil that dripped with ghee throughout the journey, leaving greasy splotches on my clothes. I had set my aims on a hike up to Gomukh, the glacier mouth of the Ganges river. The trail access to Gomukh was inaccessible most of the year, and I took a gamble by arriving at the earliest possible date of opening. After the most sobering bus journey of my life up impossibly narrow mountain roads, I arrived in a small town where all road access ended. I immediately encountered a small gaggle of international hikers who had taken the same risk as me, all of us delighted to discover the trail had indeed just opened, and we would be the first of the year to hike it. Among the multicultural crew was a lanky German photographer with a guitar who would become a beloved friend and traveling companion for a decade to come.

At the crack of dawn, I slipped on my brand-new hiking boots and set off up the mountain trail. The boots were ill-fitting deadweights that quickly tore my feet into bloody slabs. Within hours, wearing them became unbearable, so I tied them to my backpack and hiked up the mountain in flip-flops. By the time we reached the glacier, I could no longer feel my feet on the snowy trail and slid my way without traction toward the magnificent ice mouth. Awestruck by the colossal wonder, we gathered blissfully in embrace, feeling together the magnitude of the world. When darkness began to fall fast upon us, we raced down the mountain to a halfway shelter, where we huddled together on the floor like a pile of puppies, sharing our body heat throughout the night.

After Gomukh, I spent days on the back of the German's motorcycle, singing my heart out into the wind as we snaked our way through the Parvati Valley. I became aware of my lifelong tendency to brace against oncoming threat and tried to open myself to my surroundings; I wanted to love every-one, everything. Eventually we arrived at Manikaran, a pilgrimage site for Sikhs known for its hot springs and sites of worship. From Manikaran, we hiked to an ashram near Pulga, unconcerned with how long we might stay. When we arrived, we were greeted by a handful of devoted residents who boasted that the ashram had the purest flowing water in the world. It was a persuasive and persistent sell, and eventually I drank from the flowing stream—a critical error that sent my body into a state of full-throttle evacuation. After two days of intense vomiting and diarrhea, I was assisted by the German down the narrow hiking path one severely dehydrated step at a time, back to Manikaran in search of medical help.

Arriving in town, we asked the first stranger we encountered for assistance and were led to an Ayurvedic doctor. The doctor was Sikh, and learning of my heritage, he instantly welcomed me with the warmest enthusiasm. In the examination room, he expressed great interest in my father, pronouncing me a *Daughter of India* even while, as a foreigner, I had been poisoned by its purest water. *You are a child of Mother India, and so you are my child, my daughter,* he declared. *You come again tomorrow,* he said with a smile. *I will give you a special treatment to help you get well faster.*

From the future, I look back at him as the perfect villain in a cosmopolitan novel, the one who drops in to perform an act of harm and then retreats from the narrative altogether. He disappears but leaves an imprint that endures. The German rightfully found it strange and suspicious that the doctor was so keen to claim me as one of his own, and told me in no uncertain terms not to return. We fought over his suspicion, me insisting that his Western male authority was blinding him to the loving gesture of a doctor wanting to help a returned member of his tribe.

When I arrived at the office the following morning, I was weaker than I had ever been. The office appeared closed, but the doctor immediately arrived to escort me inside with his unwavering smile, shutting the door behind me. I immediately felt uneasy, the German's suspicion echoing in my mind and my already sickened gut telling me to turn back. The doctor led me into a ramshackle room quite unlike the examination room the day before. By the remnants of chai and snacks that were strewn about, I gleaned that these were his private quarters. He asked me to lay down on the table and lift my shirt so he could examine my stomach, and then he told me he was going to give me an Ayurvedic massage to move the sickness through my body. He turned on a little television off to the side of the examination table. The sound was muffled, but I glanced over and saw Indian women dancing across the screen. He watched the screen with an odd nonchalance, becoming almost uninterested in his Ayurvedic treatment. He massaged my stomach, pressing here and there as though there was some medical rhyme to his reason. Then, with his eyes still fixed on the television, he grabbed my breasts and brought his body down hard on mine. I froze for a moment, assessing the scene—him, me, the Bollywood women on the television—as though each of us might merely be actors in some fantastical perversion. I gathered strength I did not have, morphing into a feral cat refusing its capture. I writhed and clawed, twisted my body abnormally, moved swiftly and unequivocally. As I fled, the doctor feigned a great, theatrical surprise, hissing that I was a stupid Western girl as I pushed my way into the streets and wept openly, a sickly foreign spectacle.

Nathan and I have offered you a significant amount of independence in your childhood, a practice born in equal parts from our pedagogical orientation and from your inborn drive for autonomy. You never stray far, but you like to feel you are doing things independently, the comfort of your parents close, but not so close as to negotiate your every transaction with the world. Together apart, apart together: a toggle once invented to characterize my queer relationship to your father has now emerged as a style of family living.

In the grocery store one day, as you returned to me from one aisle over with a box of pasta in hand that you had proudly fetched yourself, an older woman approached us and shouted in my face: *A girl was abducted here once! You should never take your eyes off your daughter!* I wanted to respond to her rationally, to explain that the overwhelming majority of abductions were at the hands of a parent or guardian who had lost access or rights to their child, and that to boot, the likelihood of a second abduction in the same place was slim to none. I wanted to tell her that while I feared abduction as much as every other parent in this culture, that I too am supersaturated by fears of kidnapped girls, I also think it's important to return some of the freedoms and autonomies that have been stripped away from children by mainstream paranoia and its market value. Instead, I looked at her squarely and responded with a polite and deferential, *Thank you for telling me.*

In your early years, we clothed you in hand-me-downs that ranged from frilly dresses to gender-neutral tank tops and boyish terrycloth shorts. While our fashion choices were mostly practical, I admit that I loved seeing you most in tomboy attire, projecting my own youthful fashion leanings onto your tiny body. We saw no need to enforce your gender through aesthetic practices, at least in any consistent way. When you were mistaken for a boy, we rarely corrected people. It seemed entirely unnecessary, and important in your youth to loosen the stranglehold of gender. These days, your style is unabashedly girlish, informed by the gender performances at school. But at home, you like to tell me how, most often, you feel more comfortable in the realm of boys. *I look like a girl,* you tell me, *but really, I'm a half-girl, half-boy witch.* Before I can fully attach to this self-designation, you have morphed again into a creature that is *half-human, half-bat* and settled there for a long stretch. I love your embrace of hybrid identifications, your refusal to desire the treacherous fiction of purity.

You showed frustration over gender for the first time when you were four years old. At the time, you were sporting an adorably short haircut that allowed us to avoid the drama of hair brushing. At the grocery store, someone walked past us and said, *What a cute little boy!* You looked incredulous and declared loudly, *I. Am. A. Girl!* The passerby's statement was, of course, meant as a public compliment, one that had gone awry by turning the intended attention on cuteness into what felt like an insult waged against your gender identity. I knew how you felt, having been persistently mistaken for a boy across my own prepubescent youth. The experience of chronic misgendering created in me a long-lasting body confusion. Coupled with race and racial hybridity, my body felt hideous and bluntly misunderstood. This feeling did not abate in puberty, when I burst into an unequivocally feminine body, transforming rapidly from a "boyish" state to full-figured femininity. I concealed my body as much as possible, and persistently punished it

for breaching the obscenely restrictive standards of normative femininity. Gender, ultimately, made me sick.

A few minutes later, as we headed down aisle five in search
of frozen peas, you asked me why the passerby had thought
you were a boy. I explained that people look for clues to
determine gender, culled from details such as how you are
dressed or the style of your hair. You were sporting slip-on
shoes, terrycloth shorts, and a tank top, clothing that from
my perspective seemed relatively gender-neutral. Aside from
your cropped hairstyle (which seemed to me more squarely
French New Wave femme than straight masculine), it was
difficult to explain why you had been interpreted this way.
It felt important in that moment to explain to you that how
we are perceived is often misaligned with how we feel, or
how we desire to be seen.

By the time we reached the snack aisle, we had digressed
into a conversation about the power of language. We were
discussing why being misgendered can feel deeply hurtful.
By way of example, I said that being called a boy to someone who identifies as a boy would likely produce no negative effect, while being called a boy had hurt you—as it
might hurt any person who did not feel like a boy, regardless of their genitalia. You made me laugh when you suggested that in this context the word *boy* might be a *potty
word*, a term I had never heard you use before and one
that was certainly not part of our family lexicon. I understood your meaning, but told you I didn't really believe in
potty words. Words, I explained, were not bad in and of
themselves, but carried histories that require attentiveness
and sensitivity. When used in particular contexts, so-called

potty words could be construed as inappropriate, or even harmful. But in other situations, they might well create the grounds for intimacy and new or renewed forms of alliance. Overhearing part of our conversation, a mother passed us by with a child in a shopping cart and looked at me aghast. A hipster employee stocking shelves smiled at the oddity of a mother publicly denouncing the notion of bad language to her child.

A year or so later, an especially bright genderqueer student of mine came over to babysit, and the two of you set off on a much-anticipated neighborhood expedition in search of gems. When you returned home an hour later and began to sort through a bag of little stones and shiny objects, my student mentioned that you had asked them whether they were a boy or a girl, and they had answered *neither*. They commented on how wild it was that gender norms are instantiated so early in life, and wanted me to know about the conversation just in case any questions should arise.

That night in the bath, I asked you about the conversation. We had plenty of friends who had transitioned, but none at the time who identified outside of the binary. I described gender as a spectrum rather than a point of arrival while you splashed around in the tub and mulled it all over. Then you looked up at me, your hair full of suds, and said, *So my babysitter is a middle cutie?* I was immediately captivated by your ability to invent a new term and speak it with absolute conviction, as though *middle cutie* was part of a public lexicon rather than something you had invented on the spot. Not only did I love the phrase, I loved how it revealed your capacity to invent new languages for being and belonging.

I loved, also, that you had brought *cuteness* back into gender play. If the declaration of you being a cute boy had felt to you like a social affront not long ago, here you brought cuteness back into the fold, letting it demarcate a difference that is not eschewed but fully loved and embraced.

You have been reared through an explicitly Brown maternity. For now, and for the most part, your orientations stem from mine. I imagine these orientations as rhizomes sending out little shoots that will lead you far away from me. I can't even begin to anticipate where they might take you. I want to offer myself to you as a base, not so you can build yourself up from a fantasy of solid ground, but so you can discover the breaks, cracks, and sinkholes that constitute the lives that came before you. So that I might become for you a map of broken things, a recyclable archive that will spur you to fashion other ways of being alive, of living. I want to hand myself over so that you don't have to go in search of me, so you can draw forward what you need to reinvent the world.

I desire never to lose you, but for the sake of life itself, I need you to lose me. At the end of this world, you will rightfully be angry about what I am not yet prepared to reject in this age of purported freedom. But I hope your anger will not lead you to abandon everything that came before you, that it does not prevent you from culling what is of use from history for the future you will strive toward. What you retain and what you abandon will determine the very possibility of future life, its shapes and forms. To choose your inheritance will require a dedication to lose so much more than you feel capable of, to leave behind more than is bearable in the effort to live on. It will mean letting go of almost everything that, in the here and now, feels indispensable to our everyday lives.

These choices will require acts of indebted critique—of sifting through our individual and collective pasts not to burn down your ancestors for what they failed to accomplish, but to learn from what they neglected and to cull the latent seeds planted by our awe-inspiring foremothers. It is your work to selectively glean from human histories what is useful to you for another, more livable world. Indebted critique is the labor of finding what was already there but could not be fully thought or lived out within the systems that came before you. It is the act of seeking out the past—its mothers, movements, thinkers, and texts—and lovingly pilfering from them what serves a vibrant future.

Just as soon as this book is finished and finds a publishing home, a global pandemic sweeps over the world, and the book's publication is pushed years into the future. I can't help but wonder what these words will mean in that future time, whether all these pages that anticipate the end of one world will speak to the one that comes after.

It will be months yet before George Floyd is publicly executed by a police officer in the streets of Minneapolis, a uniformed knee bearing down on his throat while he says, over and over, *I can't breathe,* until he stops. Months before the nation will roil in protest, and we will witness more white people in the streets decrying racism than we have seen in our lifetimes, more than we could have imagined.

It will be months before the United Daughters of the Confederacy building will be set on fire around the corner from the duplex, when smoke will come pouring out of the windows, moving purposefully toward the newly acquired Kehinde Wiley equestrian countermonument, *Rumors of War*. The smoke will angle toward the dreadlocked Black man in Nike high-tops who is halting his horse abruptly just before reaching the smoking building. The horse is facing forward and twisting left, but the man is twisted right, looking back over his shoulder, away from the Confederate building at what's coming, what has already arrived. He is looking at the always-encroaching past, but everything about his body angles us toward a future that will, without doubt now, take us elsewhere.

At the same moment the fire is lit, orchestrated protesters will surround each of the Confederate statues on Monument Avenue, spray-painting the bases and rendering them anew. The protesters disperse quickly, leaving only their colorful traces behind. The graffiti is stunning and builds over days, turning the monuments into gorgeous collective artworks that make felt and known the politics of the present and future.

It will be months before riot police comb our streets, helicopters hovering overhead at night, before sirens throughout the city make it impossible to sleep. Months before you'll lace up your roller skates and we will head over to the monuments, stopping to see how each one changes, night after night, in contact with an exquisite public refusal. At the open concrete encasing of an absented Jefferson Davis, whose bronze body has just been pulled down by protesters and swiftly taken somewhere out of view, we stop to behold the monument without its patriarch. We are alone, the two of us, and you lean back against the monument beside the spray-painted face of George Floyd. All we do is breathe, quiet and contemplative.

In the distance, you see friends approaching—an Asian American mother and her Black son in COVID masks, whom you wave over to join us at a safe distance. You skate the roundabout a few times while the rest of us chat, when out of nowhere an aging white woman pulls her car near to us and begins to scream, *Terrorists! You're all terrorists!* She wags her arthritic finger as she points at each of our bodies. Our friend shouts back, outright refusing the force of whiteness, even from this frail old lady. *Oh, fuck you!* she roars, which is a more compact way of saying, *Lady, move on now, your time has already passed.* The old woman leaves us momentarily, only to circle back a few minutes later to heckle us more. It's as though she has found her target at last, as though she has been waiting for this day, and is finally unleashed.

When we bid farewell to our friends, we say to each other, *Stay safe,* and we know we mean both *Don't get sick* and *Don't get hurt.* There are threats in every direction. We roll on toward the Robert E. Lee monument, which has been renamed by the people the Marcus-David Peters Circle in honor of a local Black man killed by Richmond police. When we arrive at the circle, we will join a constant vigil;

we will feel, as we do each time, that the air there feels altogether different, heavy and promising.

As you skate, you remain steadfastly on the lookout for the old bird, watching every car that passes and wondering aloud if it's her. *Are we in danger, Amma?* you ask me. *No, love, that old lady can't hurt us.* As you pick up speed and I keep a quick pace, you tell me how much you loved our friend's unabashed *Fuck you!* I tell you I liked it too. The old lady's racist empowerment, yielded at the expense of our variously racialized bodies, required immediate, vocal response. You nod your head, then pivot on your roller skates and turn toward me. *What's a terrorist?* you ask curiously. *The word derives from* terror, *so it means one who causes fear. It was the woman's intention to cause us fear, and so in an odd sense, it's she who is the terrorist here.* You roll ahead fast, as though you're leaving me behind, but then circle back, using my body to stop your forward motion, hugging me at the same time.

It's still months before all this, before a diverse America will take to the streets for who knows how long in refusal of police brutality. In the months before this America, we are all in pandemic isolation, wrapping ourselves around another new world. We are living in the thickness of this moment, having become ever more aware of our own bodies, and so quickly afraid of the bodies of others. School has been canceled for weeks now, putting an abrupt halt to your life in second grade. In succumbing to the new rhythms of constant togetherness, we have seized the opportunity to abandon the school curriculum, inventing an alternative education. Nathan teaches you the history of punk rock and incorporates science experiments and mathematical equations into every mundane activity. You and I wander the alleys of the Museum District and talk about the Underground Railroad while we pick vibrant flower petals and interesting leaves to make a mandala in the backyard.

Today, by way of avoiding other humans, we are heading toward a nearby urban forest that I am discovering for the first time but that you know well through a history of summer camp adventures. Refusing the official name given to this forest, you and your campmates have renamed it the All Free Forest. *Everyone who goes there can be as free as they wish, as long as they respect the land,* you say, instructing me on how to behave. *If you don't respect the forest, the trolls and giants will chase you out.* I am eager to enter the forest, to see what forms of freedom we might discover therein. Just as the forest line comes into sight, we notice two white mounted police officers straight ahead of us on our path. Our bodies tighten, and I reach for your hand. We are both nervous about the cops, and quickly deliberate over whether we should veer right to take the long way into the forest, or follow our path and meet them head-on. One officer dismounts his horse, looking toward us invitingly. The sight of the horses in the urban space seems to lure us, and before we know it, we're patting the necks and muzzles of Milo and Scottie, animals whose lives are in service of maintaining state discipline.

I have no desire to linger there, but as you pat one of the horses and begin to chat with its female rider, I find myself asking the dismounted officer whether he has heard anything about the prospect of the city shutting down access to public parks during the pandemic. *Not as long as folks continue to keep distance,* he says, then adds, *People have a hard time thinking ahead about what might happen to them.* Despite the uneasiness I feel in contact with the police, I find myself adding to his formulation, telling him the problem is not simply a capacity to think ahead about oneself in time, but of thinking and acting synchronously toward other bodies. What I mean is that the pandemic is hailing us toward an ethics that is so much wider and more capacious than we have known, so much less divisive. He nods, but I'm not sure he understands my meaning. Then he turns to you and asks, *Do you want a photo with Scottie?* You hedge, then take your pose beside the animal. As I angle my iPhone to capture the image, I consider how to frame out the policeman. But then I notice he is sliding his body behind you and the horse, completely out of sight, as though he understands and accepts that he has no place here. I am oddly touched by his willing act of self-omission.

You are still chatting with the female officer, telling her your mother used to ride as a girl, that she is hesitant about you riding because of an accident she suffered, that you want to have your own farm one day. I am trying to edge us away, cueing you that it's time to go, but you've committed to your conversation. I turn back toward the dismounted officer and ask him if he enjoys being a mounted policeman. He responds, without missing a beat, that it has changed his life. He tells me he used to be a drug unit cop, working through brute force and intimidation. Now, he presents a friendlier public disposition, spends his days tending to and riding his horse. Then he turns to Scottie, and it's as though I'm no longer there, no longer the one he is talking to. *This guy here, this guy has changed everything for me.* He is gazing at the horse as one might a beloved life partner. He is stroking its face tenderly, with unabashed love. For a moment, it appears as though he might cry. I am stunned by the sentimentality of the scene, even while the humanity of this man is not nearly enough to make me want to stay, not even close to making me feel that your body and mine are safe in his midst.

As I draw us away from the cops, I glance back quickly to see the policeman mounting his horse, receding from our horizon. You are pulling me along in excitement, faster and faster as the forest draws near. *Let's race!* you shout. And before my feet have lifted off the grass, you're running full tilt toward the All Free Forest. You're about to disappear into the woods, into a place I've not yet been.

Works Referenced

James Baldwin, "My Dungeon Shook," from *The Fire Next Time* (Vintage International, 1993).

Ta-Nehisi Coates, *Between the World and Me* (Spiegel & Grau, 2015).

Elizabeth Castle and Christina D. King, dirs., *Warrior Women* (GOOD DOCS, 2018).

Mel Chen, *Animacies: Biopolitics, Racial Mattering, and Queer Affect* (Duke University Press, 2012).

Robin Wall Kimmerer, *Braiding Sweetgrass: Indigenous Wisdom, Scientific Knowledge, and the Teachings of Plants* (Milkweed Editions, 2013).

Saidiya Hartman, *Lose Your Mother: A Journey Along the Atlantic Slave Route* (Farrar, Strauss, and Giroux, 2007).

Julietta Singh, *No Archive Will Restore You* (Punctum Books, 2018).

Néle Azevedo, *Minimum Monument* (Chamberlain Square, Birmingham, UK, 2014).

Paulo Freire, *Pedagogy of the Oppressed* (Continuum, 2000).

M. Jacqui Alexander, *Pedagogies of Crossing: Meditations on Feminism, Sexual Politics, Memory, and the Sacred* (Duke University Press, 2006).

M. Jacqui Alexander & Chandra Talpade Mohanty, eds., *Feminist Genealogies, Colonial Legacies, Democratic Futures* (Routledge, 1997).

Sara Ahmed, *Living a Feminist Life* (Duke University Press, 2017).

Justin Phillip Reed, "Paroxysm," from *Indecency* (Coffee House Press, 2018).

Naomi Shihab Nye, "What People Do," from *Words Under the Words* (Eighth Mountain Press, 1995).

Kehinde Wiley, *Rumors of War* (Virginia Museum of Fine Arts, Richmond, VA, 2019).

LITERATURE
is not the same thing as
PUBLISHING

Coffee House Press began as a small letterpress operation in 1972 and has grown into an internationally renowned nonprofit publisher of literary fiction, essay, poetry, and other work that doesn't fit neatly into genre categories.

Coffee House is both a publisher and an arts organization. Through our *Books in Action* program and publications, we've become interdisciplinary collaborators and incubators for new work and audience experiences. Our vision for the future is one where a publisher is a catalyst and connector.

Funder Acknowledgments

Coffee House Press is an internationally renowned independent book publisher and arts nonprofit based in Minneapolis, MN; through its literary publications and *Books in Action* program, Coffee House acts as a catalyst and connector—between authors and readers, ideas and resources, creativity and community, inspiration and action.

Coffee House Press books are made possible through the generous support of grants and donations from corporations, state and federal grant programs, family foundations, and the many individuals who believe in the transformational power of literature. This activity is made possible by the voters of Minnesota through a Minnesota State Arts Board Operating Support grant, thanks to the legislative appropriation from the Arts and Cultural Heritage Fund. Coffee House also receives major operating support from the Amazon Literary Partnership, Jerome Foundation, McKnight Foundation, Target Foundation, and the National Endowment for the Arts (NEA). To find out more about how NEA grants impact individuals and communities, visit www.arts.gov.

Coffee House Press receives additional support from Bookmobile; Dorsey & Whitney LLP; Fredrikson & Byron, P.A.; Kenneth Koch Literary Estate; the Matching Grant Program Fund of the Minneapolis Foundation; Mr. Pancks' Fund in memory of Graham Kimpton; the Schwab Charitable Fund; and the U.S. Bank Foundation.

The Publisher's Circle of Coffee House Press

Publisher's Circle members make significant contributions to Coffee House Press's annual giving campaign. Understanding that a strong financial base is necessary for the press to meet the challenges and opportunities that arise each year, this group plays a crucial part in the success of Coffee House's mission.

Recent Publisher's Circle members include many anonymous donors, Patricia A. Beithon, Anitra Budd, Andrew Brantingham, Dave & Kelli Cloutier, Mary Ebert & Paul Stembler, Chris Fischbach & Katie Dublinski, Jocelyn Hale & Glenn Miller, the Rehael Fund-Roger Hale/Nor Hall of the Minneapolis Foundation, Randy Hartten & Ron Lotz, Dylan Hicks & Nina Hale, William Hardacker, Kenneth & Susan Kahn, Stephen & Isabel Keating, the Kenneth Koch Literary Estate, Cinda Kornblum, Jennifer Kwon Dobbs & Stefan Liess, the Lambert Family Foundation, the Lenfestey Family Foundation, Sarah Lutman & Rob Rudolph, the Carol & Aaron Mack Charitable Fund of the Minneapolis Foundation, Gillian McCain, Malcolm S. McDermid & Katie Windle, Mary & Malcolm McDermid, Daniel N. Smith III & Maureen Millea Smith, Peter Nelson & Jennifer Swenson, Enrique & Jennifer Olivarez, Alan Polsky, Robin Preble, Jeffrey Sugerman & Sarah Schultz, Nan G. Swid, Grant Wood, and Margaret Wurtele.

For more information about the Publisher's Circle and other ways to support Coffee House Press books, authors, and activities, please visit www.coffeehousepress.org/pages/donate or contact us at info@coffeehousepress.org.

JULIETTA SINGH is a writer and academic whose work engages the enduring effects of colonization, current ecological crisis, and queer-feminist futures. She is the author of *No Archive Will Restore You* and *Unthinking Mastery: Dehumanism and Decolonial Entanglements.* She currently lives in Richmond, Virginia, with her family.

The Breaks was designed by
Bookmobile Design & Digital Publisher Services.
Text is set in Adobe Caslon Pro.